JUBILEES OF THE LMS

Jubilees
of the LMS

JOHN F. CLAY

LONDON

IAN ALLAN

First published 1971

SBN 7110 0188 X

© Ian Allan 1971

*Published by Ian Allan Ltd, Shepperton, Surrey, and printed in the United
Kingdom by the Press at Coombelands, Addlestone, Weybridge, Surrey*

Contents

Preface

THE JUBILEES were never a class of engine to earn the superlatives. The perfect locomotive was a myth and the Jubilees could be as fallible as most and perhaps more fallible than some. The great bulk of the work of this world has, however, not been performed by men of outstanding genius and sanctity but by the ordinary people and so let it be with locomotives. The Jubilee story is the story of an ordinary class of medium-sized express engine in which a share of good and bad had been mixed. They could, at times, cause great suffering and near despair to those who toiled on their footplates or who serviced them in the sheds. Yet, like many ordinary people, they had their moments of glory when they touched the heights. Perhaps their greatest hour came in October 1937 when the engine No 5660 *Rooke* stormed over Ais Gill in record time, this is a performance which, even today, when related to the size of the engine, stands high in the annals of British steam.

In view of the Jubilees' long association with the Midland division of the LMS, it is perhaps appropriate that the writing of this outline history has fallen to the lot of members of the Leicester Railway Society for, without the powerful assistance of H. A. Gamble, the founder of the Society, the work could never have been finished. A large part of the material included in Chapter 12 of this book was compiled by H. A. Gamble with the help of voluminous notes supplied by R. N. Townsin of Peterborough and with further assistance from P. E. Fox of the Leicester Railway Society. I am grateful to K. R. Phillips and Norman Harvey for the loan of logs and to P. H. V. Banyard, Gp Capt J. N. C. Law and G. A. Yeomans for their help in the assessment of the finer points of locomotive performance.

The author is also indebted to the Public Relations and Publicity Officer of the London Midland Region and to J. Edgington for permission to inspect the files at Euston House and for assistance and photographs. I am most grateful to the Editor of the *Railway Magazine* and to Messrs Cecil J. Allen and O. S. Nock for permission to quote performance details given in British Locomotive Practice and Performance. E. S. Cox has kindly given permission for me to quote test results given in his various Ian Allan books. My thanks are due also to the various photographers especially to T. G. Hepburn who has contributed so many fine prints.

LEICESTER   JOHN F. CLAY
September, 1970

CHAPTER ONE

The ancestry of the Jubilees

THE AIM OF THE DESIGNER of the Jubilee class engines was to strengthen the second division of LMS express passenger locomotives. The heavier duties in the 1930s were being worked by the Royal Scots and the first two Pacifics were in service. These engines needed better running mates, engines which could work lighter expresses at the highest speeds, which could work the heavier loads on less exacting schedules and which could, in an emergency, deputise for a Royal Scot without fear of a serious loss of time. It was also intended to raise the standard of running on lines such as the Midland by replacing four coupled engines by a larger modern design that would permit of a general acceleration of services. It was most desirable that a variety of ageing six coupled designs from the LNWR, the L&Y, the Caledonian and the G&SWR should be replaced by a single standard type of modern express engine which would have lower costs of fuel and maintenance and would be more reliable in service. The need was partly filled by the 3cyl 4-6-0s of the "Baby Scot" or Patriot class which, in 1933/4 were gaining a high reputation on the LMS. The Jubilees were intended to be an improved version of these engines.

The most successful designs in steam locomotive history did not come as one man's single inspiration but they came from the intelligent adaptation of ideas already working well in practice to which a few new features could be added. So it was that the Jubilee class originated from the grafting of a boiler based on Swindon practice on to an engine that owed its design partly to the Derby drawing office and partly to the design staff of the North British Locomotive Company. To this blending of what were thought to be sound design features were added a few new ideas aimed, mainly, at giving the engine better availability in service. It seemed that an engine based on such an apparently sound foundation could hardly fail to succeed and the designer had such faith in inevitable success that large numbers were ordered straight from the drawing board. It will be seen that all the design features did not come up to expectations in actual practice and it is interesting to go back into history for a brief look at the various trends in design which were blended together to form the first Jubilee.

As a general purpose express engine for the LMS in the 1930s it was necessary to have a machine that could develop 1,200 indicated horsepower continuously, to sustain 1,500ihp for periods of up to half an hour and to reach a short lived maximum on a steep bank of 1,800ihp. The engine would need to be able to run at 80mph on the level with loads of 300–350 tons and, when required, to run at over 90mph downhill without fear of overheating. It would also have to be able to keep its feet well enough to climb the steepest LMS banks without slipping. The choice of a 4–6–0 type engine was an almost self evident necessity for such work and there had, in fact, been a number of 4–6–0 designs in service before World War I that came very near to the desired target of performance in many respects. In varying degrees these pre-1914 designs affected the form of the Jubilees.

There were three classes of British express passenger locomotive that, in 1914, could and sometimes did, exceed 1,500ihp. They were the GWR Stars and Saints and the LNWR Claughtons. East Coast supporters might, with justice, claim that the GN Atlantics should also be included but these engines only showed their ability to reach 1,500ihp on certain epic runs recorded in the 1930s after Gresley had fitted them with 20in cylinders and 32 element superheaters. In their 1914 form even those fitted with 24 element superheaters rarely equalled the maximum ihps of the LNWR Georges. The Churchward 4–6–0s were destined to have considerable influence on the Jubilees especially in boiler design but, although the Jubilees were intended to replace the Claughtons, little evidence of LNWR practice could be recognised in their design.

There can be no doubt as to the capacity of the Stars and Saints to reach 1,500ihp although there have been no published definitive test results. There would be few occasions when such outputs would be needed before 1914. It was Churchward policy to build engines that would perform their normal work with ease and economy. It was only at holiday times, when faced with abnormal loading, that the full potential of the Stars and Saints emerged. The Star class had four cylinders arranged so that the outside pair, set back over the rear bogie wheels, drove the middle pair of coupled wheels while the inside pair set forward drove the leading coupled axle. This arrangement was inspired by the French De Glehn compound Atlantics which had been bought for experimental running on the GWR. Churchward found that he could get equal thermal efficiency with a properly designed simple engine but he was so impressed by the smooth running of the French compounds that he adopted the divided drive 4cyl arrangement for his own Star class 4–6–0s. The Saints were two cylinder engines and here the inspiration came from the best contemporary United States practice. Many GWR engine-men considered that the Saints were better for hard pounding but the Stars were better for high speed. Both classes had the same boiler and there was no significant difference in maximum power outputs actually recorded on the road. It was in boiler design that the GWR 4–6–0s were destined to influence the Jubilee class. During the heroic years of the GWR one of Churchward's assistants was a young man named William Stanier destined later to be Chief Mechanical Engineer of the LMS. It was not merely loyalty to his former chief that led him to use an adaptation of the Churchward boiler, the choice was justified by the merit of the boiler. In actual practice, however, the difference between GWR and LMS operating conditions was to prove greater than anticipated.

We, who can look back at the history of steam with detachment and put formerly controversial issues into perspective, have no doubt about the merit of the Churchward locomotives. Since they were built further progress has been mainly in the continuation of their quality in bigger machines and in the adaptation of design to with-stand lower quality fuel and less regular servicing. In the basic criteria of thermodynamics, power per unit of size and power per unit of fuel burnt, further progress has been little more than marginal.

Despite merit which seems self-evident to us there were honest people in 1914 who thought that the technique of locomotive design had reached its zenith not at Swindon but at Crewe. The average everyday standard of work of the Churchward 4–6–0s was matched by the LNWR 4–4–0s of the George the Fifth class. It was perhaps natural that people who only saw the railways from the inside of a carriage thought that Crewe possessed some magic design formula that allowed their 4–4–0s to equal the work of larger six coupled engines on other lines. The men who wielded the shovels on LNWR footplates knew exactly where the magic really lay. With such notable runs as *Wild Duck's* classic run of 145min, pass to pass, from Willesden to MP 156 recorded by Cecil J. Allen with a load of 410 tons in 1911, it was natural that some sensational performance was expected when it was first rumoured that Crewe was to build a 4cyl 4–6–0. This keenly anticipated locomotive appeared in January 1913 as the first of the Claughton class.

The Claughton had a larger firebox, a lower working pressure but a larger superheater than the GWR Star. It was probably a cheaper engine to construct than the Swindon product. The four cylinders all drove on the leading coupled axle, an arrangement that gave even better balancing than the divided drive of the Star and which allowed more easy access to the inside motion. The design of steam passages, valves and smokebox was inferior to that of the GWR engines but it was probably better than that of the majority of its contemporaries on other lines. The GWR engines proved to be superior in many points of detailed design such as lubrication, valve rings and axle-boxes. The Claughton was an engine that required skilled and dedicated firing as did the Star and Saint but the GWR had a longer period to work up the traditional skill of their firemen. Nevertheless, the Claughton was a design of great potential capacity which only missed greatness by a narrow margin. The maximum capacity of the design was shown in dramatic fashion by two test runs made in 1913 by engine No 1159 *Ralph Brocklebank*. On the first trip a load of 435 tons was worked from Euston to Crewe, 158·1 miles in 159min (152net). An indicated horse-power of 1,617 was recorded after Northchurch Tunnel. Two days later a 360-ton train was taken from Crewe to Carlisle, 141 miles, in a net time of 140½min. Tebay troughs were passed at 69mph with a recorded ihp of 1,669 and the minimum speed at Shap Summit was 37mph.

Had the Claughtons been able to reproduce such power outputs with regularity in everyday service there would have been no need for the LMS to have looked elsewhere for their second division engine in the mid thirties. There were a few occasions before and after World War I when *Ralph Brocklebank* type running took place but such occasions were unhappily rare and the average everyday standard of running was little better than that of the four coupled engines. As shopping times drew near the falling off in performance was considerable and coal consumption rose. This was partly due to the leakage of steam past the single wide type Schmidt piston valve ring. If a full comparison of the work of the Claughton and the Star is made, including points awarded for consistency of performance, speed and economy, then there is little doubt that the honours would rest with Swindon but if the sole criterion is maximum horse-power then the *Ralph Brocklebank* figures were never surpassed by Star or Saint. Before 1914 it was an almost certain fact that the Claughton's 1,669ihp was a British record but, in fairness, it has to be added that *Ralph Brocklebank* was deliberately extended to find the maximum horse-power. The coal consumption was not even measured. Contemporary tests carried out on the GWR were rather to investigate the economy of the engine at normal rates of working. If a Star or a Saint had been driven as hard size for size as, for example, King class engine No 6001 on controlled road tests in 1953, then something very close to the Claughton maximum would, doubtless, have been recorded.

The Jubilee class had three cylinders and this feature was not adopted from either GWR or LNWR practice. The 3cyl engine was the subject of a patent by Isaac Dodds in 1839 and a 3cyl single driver engine was built by Robert Stephenson and Co in 1846. In 1909 a GCR Atlantic No 1090 was rebuilt with three cylinders and it ran in this form until 1922. It would be straining credulity to suggest that the Jubilees were influenced by any of these three cylinder simple engines but it is necessary to mention them as a matter of historical coincidence.

The locomotive world of the days before World War I was a very different place from that of the 1930s but an intelligent observer of steam locomotive design and performance, asked in 1914 to forecast the design trends that would influence the form of a 4–6–0 to be used on the LNWR in 20 years time, would have been very surprised to learn how standards of values were to change and how little of the LNWR tradition, so highly esteemed in 1914, would be thought to be worthy of consideration in 1934.

CHAPTER TWO

The troubled early years of the LMS

As PEACE RETURNED after World War I it became apparent that the world in which the railway industry had prospered had gone, never to return. Operating costs had risen and although road transport had hardly reached the point of being able to inflict mortal damage, it was eating its way into railway receipts. There is no doubt that complete bankruptcy lay ahead for some of the companies and yet no one in the early '20s had the temerity to suggest that the nation could do without its railways. The solution proposed was that the railways were to be grouped into four large concerns allowing for the economies of large scale operation and shielding the more vulnerable companies by the strength of the more prosperous. A similar process has been followed in forms of business other than the railways right up to this day and whatever economies have resulted there has also been a good deal of human misery involved.

Following the grouping of 1923 the LMS, the largest group, suffered the most from conflicting loyalties and thwarted ambitions and its locomotive department in particular took longer than most to settle down. The enthralling story of those troubled years has been graphically told by E. S. Cox in some of his excellent books published by Ian Allan Ltd in recent years. The LNWR had been a proud concern; almost a part of the British establishment and before 1914 it had seemed as permanent as the Navy or Empire. Just as the Battle of Jutland had shown that the proud British battle cruisers could be mortal, the strains of the postwar period showed the fallibility of the loud voiced creations of Crewe. C. J. Bowen Cooke, the designer of the Claughtons, had died in 1920 and following the preliminary amalgamation of the LNWR and L&Y railways the post of CME had gone to George Hughes of the L&Y by seniority. This particular ascendency by the smaller partner seemed inexplicable to Crewe but Hughes was an able, broad-minded engineer and, had he been able to have carried all his ideas through to their logical conclusion, he might have made a most favourable impact on the general locomotive position. In the larger amalgamation of 1923 Midland officers took many of the higher administrative posts and the operating department fell largely under Midland influence. Conflict between the design and operating departments became intense and progress in locomotive design was the first battle casualty.

Hughes adopted the superheated version of his own 4cyl 4–6–0, nicknamed the "Dreadnoughts", as the first standard heavy express engine pending the development of a Pacific. There were some good features in the L&Y engine but its efficiency was bedeviled by defects of detail such as the leakage of steam past the piston valves and this was not corrected until long after Hughes had retired and, by then, no one was very interested in his engines. The Hughes Dreadnoughts looked well in the new LMS red and, for a short time they appeared proudly on posters as part of the publicity of the new company. They worked mainly north of Crewe sharing the road over Shap with the Claughtons. Their average performance in the years 1923–27 was probably at least as good as that of the LNWR engines but they never produced individual epics of haulage equal to the best of prewar Claughton performance. The smaller grates of these engines, 27sq ft against 30·5sq ft for the Claughton, limited their ultimate power output.

It is to be regretted that the proposed Hughes Pacific was never built. This engine was to have had a 42sq ft grate area and 4cyls, it would have been at least as good as the original pair of Gresley Pacifics and it would have raised LMS prestige. There would certainly have been troubles at first but with the passing of the years there is no reason to have doubted that something akin to a Duchess would ultimately have been developed from the original design. The Midland dominated operating department, however, were thinking in terms of short trains and many of them each hauled by a Midland compound 4–4–0. The Pacific project was dropped. After the retirement of Hughes the post of CME went to a Midland man, Sir Henry Fowler and Derby hoped that this Midland victory would bring peace. It soon transpired that the idea of a frequent service of fast, light trains, however appropriate to Midland conditions, was not to be a success on the LNWR main line and a design of ample reserve power would be needed for the Anglo-Scottish services which were not competing with success against the East Coast trains. This crying need Sir Henry Fowler sought to fill, at first by a 4–6–0 version of the Midland 3cyl compounds and later by a 4cyl compound Pacific comparable in size and power with the Breville Super Pacifics whose work on the Calais–Paris Boat Trains was the admiration of locomotive engineers the world over.

The operating department, not perhaps without good reason,

shrank from the daunting prospect of a long period of growing pains as the compound Pacifics settled to their work and a long period of training needed to accustom the men to such complicated machines. GWR prestige was high at that time following their success in the exchange trials with the LNER in 1925 and, in late 1926, Castle class engine No 5000 *Launceston Castle* appeared on LNWR metals for a period of trial running. The good running of the Castle and its easy mastery over the heaviest tasks it was set on the LNWR confirmed the running department's idea that a good modern 4–6–0 was all that was required. They stipulated 3cyls as a further simplification as compared with the 4cyl Castle. Little more than the general scheming took place at Derby, the detailed design work was almost all carried out by the North British Locomotive Company of Glasgow. It was appropriate, in view of the Scottish influence on design, that the first engine was named *Royal Scot*. The LMS had, at last, a modern large 3cyl 4–6–0 comparable in size and efficiency with the best that the other three groups had to offer. The *Royal Scot* had three cylinders arranged with the outside pair driving the middle coupled axle and the inside cylinder driving the front driving axle. Access to the inside motion was restricted and in this the Claughton was far superior. The story of the Royal Scots as such lies outside the Jubilee story but they were to have a considerable influence on the Stanier design.

The North British Locomotive Company completed the Royal Scot design and built the first 50 engines with commendable speed. They settled to work, not without some growing pains but they soon showed themselves well ahead of anything else on the LMS in power and efficiency in service. A brilliant child, far outstripping its fellows, can be an embarrassment in a class and a locomotive class which stands head and shoulders above its contemporaries also poses problems. There was a great need for a secondary type of engine closer to Royal Scot competence on the main line. Had the average Claughton performance been nearer to the best they could produce all would have been well. In fact it was rarely that a Royal Scot was pressed to the *Ralph Brocklebank* level of power output. During the 1926 strike some Claughtons rose to great heights. In the August 1926 *Railway Magazine* Cecil J. Allen described a run by No 808 hauling a load of 505 tons, the 86·9 miles from Stafford to Bletchley were run in 89min 35sec. This was running of the best test quality but a wide gap yawned between such running and the average Claughton performance. The coal consumption of the Claughtons was popularly supposed to be very heavy but if it was related to the

No 45564 *New South Wales* makes
a vigorous start from Gloucester
Eastgate with a northbound train on
Sunday June 17, 1962.
[M. Pope

THE BRISTOL-
BIRMINGHAM MAIN
LINE

GWR Star class 4–6–0 *Morning Star* at Nottingham Victoria on special train in September 1937.

[T. G. Hepburn

THE ANCESTRY OF THE JUBILEES

Above: Former LNWR 4–6–0 Claughton No 5913 *Colonel Lockwood* at Willesden.

[T. G. Hepburn

Below: Claughton No 6023 *Sir Charles Cust* rebuilt with enlarged boiler and Caprotti valves at Crewe.

[T. G. Hepburn

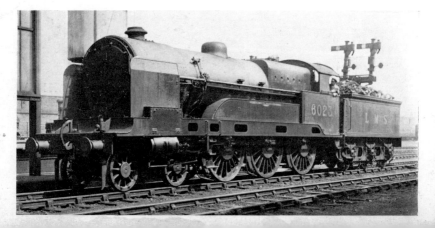

Rebuilt Claughton with large boiler
and three cylinders, later to be known
as the Patriot class. This engine has
the original Claughton wheel centres
and no deflector plates. Photographed
at Nottingham in 1931.   [*T. G. Hepburn*

THE

PATRIOTS

No 5933 of the "Baby Scot" class,
later to be known as the Patriots,
near Edwalton with the up "Thames-
Forth Express" in 1934.   [*T. G. Hepburn*

Top: Official photograph of the original No 5552, later 5642, with narrow high sided tender. This tender entered regular service with No 5607.
[*British Railways*

Above: No 5616 with original dome-less boiler and unlined narrow high sided tender. Photographed at Derby.
[*T. G. Hepburn*

THE FIRST

JUBILEES

Below: No 5557 at Crewe with wide Stanier tender and shortened chimney.
[*T. G. Hepburn*

work done it was probably no worse than other contemporary simple engines of the LMS group. After the fitting of narrow ring piston valves the Claughton tested in 1930 proved no worse than a Midland compound in coal/dhp/hr but the Claughtons were far more expensive in repair costs than the best Midland and Caledonian engines. Overheating was a constant worry and the fear of this affected running and the poor availability affected running expenses.

In all fairness it must be said that the Midland dominated LMS did their best to make something worth while out of the Claughtons. There was a strong Crewe lobby led by H. P. M. Beames fighting for their retention and the need for an engine of Claughton size was dire. The first step to revitalisation was the fitting of Caprotti gear to No 5908. This resulted in higher cylinder efficiency but the engine still stood some way short of *Launceston Castle*. At about the same time Derby tackled boiler design and 5923 had its tube layout modified to give better circulation and a better supply of air through ashpan and grate was provided. At a later date there were further experiments with the single Kylala blastpipe and with narrow ring piston valves. It was the engine with the modified valve rings which made the most sensational advance in efficiency within the original Claughton design. On test in 1930 engine No 6001 returned a coal/ dbhp/hr figure of 3·61 lb, equal to the best recorded over the same route by the famous Midland compound No 1008, the "Flower of the Flock". None of these alterations however had the slightest effect on the heavy repair bill of the Claughtons.

Following the partial success of the modified boiler on No 5923 a new enlarged boiler with a working pressure of 200 lb against the original 175 lb was designed. This boiler was of greater diameter and it made the engine look far more powerful. In 1928 a total of 20 engines were rebuilt with the new boiler, half of the class had Caprotti poppet valve gear and the remainder had Walschaerts gear and piston valves. These engines were given the duties next in difficulty to those handled by the Royal Scots including the heavy "Irish Mail". They proved rather better in everyday service than the unaltered Claughtons in those days though it is doubtful if one ever equalled the best prewar test performances. The engine with the Walschaerts gear and narrow ring piston valves showed slightly better economy on test than the engine with Caprotti gear. The figure of 3·25 lb/dbhp/hr was excellent and almost equal to the best recorded by a Royal Scot. It showed forcibly how near to greatness the Claughtons had always been. The repair cost bill was however a great disappointment and despite their almost exclusive employ-

B

ment on top link duties with special attention, they proved almost as expensive to maintain as the original Claughtons. The rebuilding had helped but it had not provided a complete solution to the problem of finding a suitable engine to reinforce the ranks of the Royal Scots.

In 1930 Derby tackled the problem in a radical manner, the enlarged Claughton boiler was considered to be a success and the Royal Scots had, by then, settled to reliable and satisfactory work. The rebuilt Claughton boiler was therefore mated with the chassis of a Royal Scot making a smaller edition of the Scots with a wider radius of use owing to reduced axle loading. A number of Claughton parts were kept in the first two engines Nos 5902 and 5971 but the later members of the class were unrepentantly new engines though given the courtesy title of "accountants rebuilds". The efficiency of the new engines on test proved to be even better than the best of the 4cyl rebuilds and the repair bill was reduced in dramatic fashion. A total of 52 engines were built in this class and they were well received everywhere they were sent. The unofficial nickname of "Baby Scots" was given to the class but it was deprecated in official circles as lacking in dignity. The LNWR War Memorial had been a Claughton class engine named *Patriot* when this engine became due for scrapping a correspondent in the *Railway Magazine* asked that the name should continue on a more modern engine. The authorities grasped at the opportunity and the name *Patriot* was given to a "Baby Scot" with the suggestion that the class be henceforth known as the Patriot class and the nickname forgotten. The unofficial title lingered for a time but finally official persistence prevailed and as the Patriot class they became generally known. They were destined to be a major influence on the Jubilee design.

CHAPTER THREE

The Patriots set a high standard

IN THE EARLY 1930s a distinct style of locomotive was becoming symbolic of the LMS. The new LMS house style was exemplified by the Royal Scots and the Patriots for express passenger work, by the Horwich Moguls, known as the Crabs, for mixed traffic work, by the elegant and very efficient 2300 class 2–6–4Ts and by the 2–6–2Ts which looked so much like the 2–6–4Ts but, owing to poor valve and front end design, lacked their moral fibre. These were, perhaps, not all very handsome engines but they had a business-like appearance and superficially at least it looked as if the LMS had at last found the way ahead. Behind the scenes however the old rivalries remained and all was not well.

The early 1930s saw the country suffering the miseries of a severe economic depression. The railways, which depended so much on the heavy industries, shared in the general gloom. There had been changes in the LMS higher command and the head man was now the well known economist Sir Josiah Stamp who instituted a policy of ruthless economy. The locomotive situation was a major worry. The modern LMS types formed but a small percentage of the total stock. Many engines were growing old, many were too small and most of them cost too much to run and maintain. Above all there were too many types each needing spare parts. Sir Josiah Stamp looked for a man of strong character who could over-rule the warring factions and could put through a ruthless programme of scrapping and replacement by modern designs which would reduce running costs and allow the desired acceleration programme to take place.

At the end of 1930 it was announced that Sir Henry Fowler was to take up a research post which meant in effect that he left the locomotive department. The post of CME was given to E. J. H. Lemon who formerly had charge of the Carriage and Wagon Department. This proved to be merely an administrative appointment pending the selection of a suitable man to carry out the drastic restocking. At this time the reputation of the GWR was at its zenith. Swindon engines had scored heavily in exchange running on the LNER in 1925 and on the LMS in 1926, in 1927, the Kings had appeared and by 1930 they were working very heavy loads on the West of England main line with conspicuous success while in 1931 the Castles set up new high speed records on the "Cheltenham Flyer". Above all however the GWR, thanks to the forward looking policy of Churchward, had a full range of standard modern types such as Sir Josiah Stamp wanted for the LMS. It was therefore with no surprise but with mixed feelings that the LMS men learned that W. A. Stanier, the second man at Swindon, was to move to the LMS as CME from January 1, 1932.

The appointment of Mr Stanier on January 1 did not mean that on January 2 taper boilers and copper capped chimneys would flood the LMS. The changes which were now foreshadowed would take time but meanwhile the best use would have to be made of the existing LMS engines. The summer of 1932 saw the introduction of a notable programme of acceleration, mainly on the former LNWR main line. The Up "Mancunian" was retimed to a 61·9mph average from Wilmslow to Euston while the 5.25pm up Liverpool express was booked at 64·5mph from Crewe to Willesden. The brunt of the new fast running fell to the Royal Scots but as more Patriots came into service their value as suitable engines for the fastest bookings was abundantly demonstrated.

There had been some indication of the efficiency of the 3cyl rebuilds, classed as 5XP along with the 4cyl enlarged boilered Claughtons, in a series of dynamometer car trials in the summer of 1931. The trains selected were Euston–Manchester expresses loaded to around 410 tons tare and booked at the relatively moderate average speed of 52·7mph. The results were as follows:

4cyl Walschaerts gear	38·2 lb/mile	3·25 lb/dbhp/hr
4cyl Caprotti gear	39·9 lb/mile	3·53 lb/dbhp/hr
3cyl Patriot	35·2 lb/mile	3·12 lb/dbhp/hr

The difference in coal consumption per unit of work done was not sensational and the Claughton with the Walschaerts gear and narrow ring piston valves showed up remarkably well, again hinting at what the Claughton class might have been with better detailed design. When the repair costs could also be examined it was found that the 3cyl engines had reduced these costs by almost 50per cent. This fully justified the greater capital cost of a rebuilding which was really a replacement.

Stanier decided that one of his standard designs would be an engine corresponding to the GWR Castle or Star but he found material already ordered for a series of Patriots. The new engines were badly needed and their construction was allowed to proceed with minor improvements in detail such as axleboxes. These were the engines destined to raise the reputation of the "Baby Scot", later to be called the Patriot class, to great heights in the next few years. They were to prove themselves some of the fastest engines that had, up to that time, run on LMS metals.

The LMS was not a fast railway in 1931 and the reputation of the Royal Scots had to be gained mainly by long non-stop running, by heavy load haulage, and by sturdy hill climbing. The accelerations of 1932 revealed a new facet to their performance. In the autumn of 1932 the LMS ran some high speed specials for motor dealers travelling to and from Coventry. On the return journey Tring Summit was passed at 69 and 72mph respectively by engines 6100 and 6109 with 305-ton trains. Hitherto the speed honours had been held mainly by the GWR with the hint of challenge to come from the Gresley Pacifics but now it became apparent that the LMS did not intend to remain for ever out in the cold. The publicity departments of the GWR and the LNER had realised that the public liked to have its heroes and the names of drivers such as W. Sparshatt of Kings Cross and J. W. Street of Old Oak Common sheds had become well known. A driver who took a share in the running of the Coventry specials was Driver L. A. Earl of Camden, a man short of stature but great in heart, who was destined to become as famous as any. It was with Patriot class engines that the great Laurie Earl performed some of his finest runs.

On October 18, 1932 the accelerated Up "Mancunian" was loaded to 12 bogies of 355 tons tare, 375 tons full and was hauled by Patriot class engine No 5959 driven by L. A. Earl. The non-stop run from Wilmslow was cut short at Polesworth where the train had to stop because of injector trouble. The fault was rectified and the train set off again with 92min remaining for the 106½ miles. The feat was actually accomplished but, owing to an over cautious brake application, the initial stop was well short of the buffers. Drawing up took three more minutes, but as far as locomotive performance is concerned, the driver had succeeded in recovering his lost time. The start to stop run had been made at an average of 69mph, the 77 miles from Rugby, passed at reduced speed, to Willesden had taken 61min while from Roade to Willesden 54½ miles were run in 41min at an average of 80mph. It is a thousand pities that no experienced train timer was on board to record speeds in detail. The guard's journal figures are approximate but something within the general pattern must have taken place and such times would inevitably demand a minimum speed of around 70mph at Tring and maxima of 90mph at Castlethorpe and on the descent from Tring to Euston. The standard of running, in view of the heavier load, surpassed the Royal Scots on the Coventry specials but in fairness it must be recorded that in the following year the Royal Scot class engine *Comet* improved considerably on the 1932 timings.

It appears that No 5959 was a most lively engine because shortly after she was on the Up "Lancastrian" which was routed via Stoke and had the substantial load of 14 bogies and a small van totalling 445 tons. The engine was in charge of Longsight men Driver Rogers and Fireman Lennarddo who was shortly to appear on the BBC programme *In Town Tonight* because of his talent as a singer. From an out of course stop at Nuneaton the 97·1 miles to Euston took 93min 26sec. The 69·9 miles from Welton to Willesden had been covered at an average speed of 70·7mph and Tring was passed at 61mph. When designing the GWR 4–6–0s Churchward set himself the target of a drawbar pull of 2 tons at 70mph; No 5959 had approached the target for an hour.

It was the normal practice of some of the top link men in those days, when working fast up trains, to make their maximum effort on the superb piece of road from Welton to Willesden and this type of high speed work on easy gradients was to the liking of Patriot class engines in their youth. The Up 5.25pm from Liverpool hauled by No 5517 with 325 tons in charge of Driver Earl averaged 76·8 from Welton to Wembley passing Tring at 72mph. The Patriots took over the harder Birmingham duties from the compounds and Driver Earl with No 5925 with 270 tons ran from Coventry to Willesden in a net time of 76¾min for the 88·6 miles while an even better run was made by 5551, the last Patriot to be built, on a dynamometer car test with 330 tons and a net time of 76¼min. In the 1947 edition of *Trains Annual* Driver Earl wrote a reminiscent article in which he claimed that the Patriots were faster engines than the larger Royal Scots.

On the Midland the Patriots showed a similar performance pattern to that on the LNWR. They showed up to best advantage at high speeds. With the Patriots 90mph maxima were recorded for the first time since the days of Charles Rous Marten. The 5XP class 4–6–0s were used frequently on the Scottish express leaving St Pancras at 12noon and booked 72min over the 68·9 miles from Luton to Leicester. They showed their ability to cut this to 66½min with 10 bogies of 330 tons. On a misty autumn day in 1934 I travelled down to Leicester on the 12noon with No 5505 at the head of 9 bogies. The evening before I had listened to Cecil J. Allen's graphic account of the running of Sparshatt and 4472 on the Leeds high speed special. Thoughts ran to high speeds as 5505 reached a near 90mph maximum before Bedford, topped Sharnbrook at 51mph and reached Leicester in 68½min. At Luton we passed an up express headed by a compound piloted by a 2–4–0. This seemed symbolic of the old Midland that was passing while our own engine represented the new more vigorous LMS. The Patriot came off at Leicester and worked a semi-fast to Nottingham before returning to St Pancras on an up express via Melton. Impecunious sixth formers around Leicester who are now among the elder statesmen of railway societies invested in cheap day returns to Loughborough in order to sample the new 4–6–0s.

On the heavier grades over Shap, over Ais Gill and in Scotland the 5XPs acquitted themselves well but they did not surpass the compounds by the same margin of superiority that they showed on their high speed flights. The compounds were at their best in slogging up heavy grades and despite rumours, they were never exceptionally fast. The modern valve and front end design of the Patriots made them very suitable for the same type of high speed running that had made the GWR Stars so famous.

The success of the Royal Scots and the Patriots gave the LMS engineers the evidence to make a strong case for 3cyl propulsion in new designs. The new CME had come from the GWR which used only 2 or 4cyl engines. It would have been natural for Stanier to have been a little suspicious of 3cyl engines but the good running of the Patriots could not be ignored.

CHAPTER FOUR

The first Jubilee

IT IS PERHAPS difficult for us, looking back and seeing the history of the steam locomotive in perspective, to imagine that there ever was a time when that distinguished locomotive engineer, the late Sir William Stanier FRS could ever have been the subject of criticism, Yet, in mid-1934, when the first engine of the class later to be known as the Jubilees appeared, he was hardly in an established position. At first he had continued to completion a number of left overs from the previous regime then he had shown his own ideas in the two prototype Pacifics, his taper boilered version of the basic 2-6-0 mixed traffic engine and his 3cyl 2-6-4s for the Tilbury line. The Pacifics at first had their fair share of growing pains and the early performance records of these engines presented little to challenge the best efforts of the GWR Kings and the LNER A3 Class Pacifics. It was into a world of mingled hopes and frustrations that the first Stanier 3cyl 5XP class 4-6-0 made its entrance.

The demands for ruthless economy instilled into the LMS by its new President of the Executive and Chairman of the Company, Sir Josiah Stamp, decreed that the number of locomotive types was to be drastically reduced. This meant that a large number of ageing engines of doubtful economy were to be hastened to the scrapheap and their work was to be performed by a smaller number of more efficient modern engines. The intention was to take full advantage of the new designs by instituting long distance inter divisional workings which would take the engines, in the hands of different crews, on extensive round circuits in England and Scotland. The new engines both of the proposed 3cyl express type and the 2cyl mixed traffic type of 4-6-0, were to work both express passenger and freight trains as required. Britain sought a compromise between the locomotive policy of the US with its emphasis on the availability of its huge stoker fired locomotives and the one man one engine policy still retained on some of the French railways with their complicated hand fired compounds running moderate daily mileages but giving superb performance and fuel economy. A policy of seeking compromise may well be very wise but it invites the criticism of those who, unrealistically, expect the best of both worlds.

In its essential conception the new 5XP was to make the standard of running shown by the parallel boilered "Baby Scot" or Patriot class engines, exemplified on the LNWR main line, available all over the LMS. To achieve this end a boiler based on the best GWR practice was mated with the chassis of the existing LMS engine while detailed modifications, destined to improve availability, were introduced. There must have been some heart searching by a designer coming from Swindon as to whether the GWR pattern of 4cyl engine should not have replaced the 3cyl LMS system completely but by using the Royal Scot and Patriot as a basis there could be a useful reduction in the number of new non-standard parts and this would appeal to the accountants. It had been announced early in 1934 that a taper boilered version of the 3cyl 5XP was to be expected and it was not difficult to visualise the new engine. Its initial impact was not sensational.

The official side view photograph, which was the first most of us saw of the new design, was not flattering, but a three-quartered side view published later was little better. There were small design faults, hardly significant from the point of view of performance, that spoilt the appearance to a disproportionate degree. The taper boiler seemed to be a blatant and aggresive feature. Where the boiler of a GWR Castle seemed to fit the engine as if it belonged, a boiler of similar size on the LMS engine seemed to be an exaggeration. It may have been that the raised running plate of the LMS engine accentuated the degree of taper or it may merely have been that what we expected on a GWR engine seemed alien to our ideas of the LMS. The GWR supporters advised their LMS friends to wait and see how much better the new engine would be but LMS supporters needed more evidence.

The taper boiler was of American origin. Its aim was to allow the best use to be made of available weight. Early American track was often of flimsy construction and the traditional 4–4–0, so familiar to cinema goers, was designed to save weight. It often had a taper boiler so exaggerated as to be almost a caricature but by the time that Churchward decided that the taper boiler was worth adapting for British conditions it had assumed a more restrained shape. By having a boiler larger at the rear end it was possible to concentrate the greatest depth of water near the firebox, the hottest part of the boiler. The firebox was the heart of a steam engine and Churchward had given a great deal of thought to its shape in order to get the most free circulation of water and to have the minimum of trouble from broken stays, cracks and leakage. This valuable experience was incorporated in the design of the new LMS engine. The taper boiler, with its carefully shaped firebox, was expensive to build but it was hoped that it would be cheaper to maintain. In view of the desire for cheap maintenance it is strange that the working pressure was raised to 225lb against the 200lb of the Patriot. The theory supporting the use of the tapered boiler seems to be a logical one but, in fairness, it must be recorded that the simple round topped parallel boiler fitted to the LNER B1 class 4-6-0s was the equal in evaporation to the taper boilered Class 5 engines of LMS, GWR and BR design.

A good feature of the Stanier boiler was the more generous width of the spaces between inner and outer fireboxes known as the firebox water legs. This was a distinct advance on the LMS parallel boilered 5XP. The GWR boilers had no steam domes, the steam was collected from a perforated pipe above the firebox and the regulator valve was placed in the smokebox. Instead of a dome there was a rudimentary casing incorporating the top feed. Top feed was a GWR feature introduced to the LMS and after a few detailed alterations it worked well. The idea was to introduce the feed water into the boiler as a spray from above rather than as a cold stream at one specific point.

The advantages gained at the rear end of a taper boiler cause troubles at the front end which, by necessity, has to be smaller in diameter. This means that there is less room for the location of a superheater of adequate size and it restricts the space available for tubes. The free gas area through which the hot gases passed from firebox to smokebox, expressed as a percentage of the grate area, was 13per cent against a desirable 15per cent. The smokebox was cylindrical in shape and was supported by a saddle. This was a real advance on the built up type used on the Royal Scot and the Patriot. It was not until after World War II that the general public began to get hints that all had not been well with the Derby type of smokebox and its replacement by the Swindon pattern was fully vindicated. This feature may well be the greatest single advance over the Patriot. Inside the smokebox GWR design prevailed, the blastpipe and chimney proportions were based on Swindon practice. The blastpipe was fitted with the Churchward jumper top, this consisted of a ring which lifted when the engine was working hard exposing a row of holes which eased the blast and reduced back pressure. In 1934 this device was held in high respect but in later years it was removed even from GWR engines.

The GWR practice of moderate superheat was followed. The theory was that there was no need to raise the temperature to a higher degree than that needed to avoid condensation at working pressure, if any higher temperature was used it meant that heat was thrown to waste up the chimney and the dryer steam raised lubrication problems. Again in 1934 this seemed to be sound reasoning and the excellent performance of GWR engines with moderate superheat could be quoted in support but again in later years Swindon changed its policy.

The taper boiler was placed on an engine which was basically of the standard Royal Scot or Patriot 3cyl design. This was designed partly by the LMS and partly by the North British Locomotive Company. The two outside cylinders drove the middle pair of driving wheels while the inside cylinder drove the leading axle. The inside cylinder and motion was inaccessible but this was no worse than the inside cylinders of the GWR 4cyl 4-6-0s. The unequal length of the connecting rods of inside and outside cylinders was a point of criticism. When Edward Thompson sought to supersede the Gresley system, of all three cylinders driving the middle axle, by divided drive he went to extreme lengths to keep the connecting rods of equal length. This raised other problems and the engines achieved only moderate success. His successor A. H. Peppercorn adopted the same layout as that used on the LMS 3cyl engines with better results. It is doubtful if the relatively short inside connecting rod was ever a serious disadvantage. There was a small difference in valve travel $6\frac{1}{8}$in for the inside cylinder and $6\frac{3}{8}$in for the outside pair. This was doubtless to compensate for the different lengths of rod but in practice wear in the motion may well have made nonsense of such a small difference.

The higher boiler pressure of 225lb/sq in against 200lb/sq in gave no intrinsic advantage but it did allow the cylinders to be reduced to 17in diameter from the 18in of the Patriots. The same 9in diameter piston valves were retained so the valve/cylinder ratio was larger suggesting a faster engine. This of course was only one factor influencing speed, the LNER A4s had 9in piston valves with $18\frac{1}{2}$in cylinders and in practice proved faster than anything on the GWR, the LMS or the SR.

The new engine was improved in many features of mechanical design. The Swindon axlebox gave better performance than the Derby type but Stanier by improving on Swindon practice went further than either. The wheels were fitted with the Gibson ring of triangular section to fasten the tyres and fractured tyres, which could be nerve racking in service, became a thing of the past. The balance weights for the coupled wheels were built up by steel plates on both sides of the spokes and riveted, the requisite weight was provided by filling in between the plates with lead. The coupling and connecting rods were of high tensile manganese molybdenum steel, the connecting rods were of fluted section and the coupling rods of rectangular section. The standard type of four wheeled bogie was adopted. The weight was taken by side bolsters and side spring gear was provided to give smooth riding. The Jubilees in general retained a better reputation for smooth riding than most of the contemporary 4–6–0s on LMS or LNER metals.

The cab was of the same general pattern as that used by Stanier on his new Pacifics and Moguls. It followed the Horwich pattern rather than the modified Midland pattern used by Fowler. There were two sliding windows on each side and hinged windows were provided on the front plate. On each side of the cab there was a small hinged window which acted as a draught preventer for the enginemen. Tip up seats rather similar to the GWR pattern were provided on each side of the cab. The drive was on the left hand side and the controls were officially said to be arranged for comfortable handling though some footplate men suggested that comfort was a relative term. A steam brake was provided on the coupled wheels, this was operated by the drivers vacuum brake valve. A vacuum pump driven by the crosshead was provided on the left hand side of the engine. Vacuum pumps were features of LNWR and GWR locomotives but they were removed from Jubilee class engines after a short time and from the Royal Scots while later Jubilees never had them.

Inside the cab a steam manifold was mounted on top of the firebox doorplate and this was fitted with a main shut off valve. The manifold provided the necessary valves for the ejector, and steam brake, the injectors, carriage warming, whistle, pressure gauge and sight feed lubricator to regulator. The exhaust steam injector was on the fireman's side and the live steam injector on the other side. The whistle was mounted horizontally in front of the cab over the firebox top. It was of Caledonian pattern and at first enthusiasts in the English Midlands were very excited at the new sound but in a very short time it became very familiar. The regulator was incorporated in the superheater header in the smokebox but this was a feature destined to be discarded. The sanding gear of the mechanical trickle type applied in front of the leading wheels and in front and behind the middle coupled wheels. A water de-sanding apparatus was provided to clean the rails of sand after use in forward or reverse direction so preventing interference with track circuits. The carriage warming apparatus was of the standard LMS type.

The first engine of the class had an ugly tender. This was basically the standard Midland tender with 3,500 gallons of water but with raised side sheets to carry more coal. The aim of the new design was to be able to run 400 miles without visiting the coal stage but this aim was not always realised in practice. The tender was narrower than the cab and this looked very dangerous for the crew especially when viewed from the rear. This was a continuation of the LMS practice which started with the Horwich Moguls and followed with the Royal Scots and Patriots. The initial cause of the practice was the change from the Horwich influence under Hughes to the Midland influence under Fowler. The Mogul design was virtually complete at the changeover but Fowler insisted in using the maximum number of standard Midland components, the largest one being the tender which fitted the Horwich engine very badly. This continued with the Royal Scots and Patriots and with the first Jubilee but the promise of better things came with the Jubilees because it was announced that later engines of the class, those built by the North British Locomotive Company, were to have new standard 4,000 gallon tenders extended to the full width of the cab. Later some Jubilees received Royal Scot tenders as the new tenders and these were considered to be more appropriate for the larger engines. The letters LMS were not placed centrally on the tender, being nearer the rear and not in line with the letters on the cab side. These were small points but they could so easily have been improved with better results to the appearance of the engine.

It was announced that 113 engines of the new class were to be built straight from the drawing board and, in some quarters, there was criticism of this because of the risks involved. Events were destined to prove that it would have been wiser to have tested prototypes before committing the company to so much capital expenditure but, in 1934, as the first engine took the road, these risks seemed minimal. The GWR 4-6-0s were at their magnificent zenith of performance and the Royal Scots and Patriots were running well. It seemed that nothing could go wrong in the combination of such well tried practices. As the first Stanier 3cyl 5XP 4-6-0 backed on to its first train no one was worried.

CHAPTER FIVE

A disappointing start

AT FIRST little firm news came to light about the performance of the
new Stanier 3cyl 5XPs but, as they they increased in numbers,
enthusiasts had the evidence of their own eyes. In Leicester we
watched the arrival of the 12noon from St Pancras and found that
Patriot class engines often ran in early and on one notable occasion
we saw a new Stanier 2cyl mixed traffic 4–6–0 run in well before
time in about 65min start to stop for the 68·9 miles from Luton. We
noticed also that the 3cyl Stanier engines at best seemed just about
able to scrape in to time as did the compounds while sometimes
they were well down on schedule. At first we thought this could be
no more than coincidence and was merely the result of bad luck with
the signals. Gradually, in early 1935, evidence accumulated that other
lineside observers were finding the same thing was true. We began
to ask drivers and we got some very forthright replies with rather
more of a unanimous voice than was usually the case. The same
general theme ran through all the replies. "The black-uns are all
right but the red-uns won't steam". We asked our friends in the
Nottingham area and found the same general opinion, one driver
said "They are only hot water engines". Trips to Nuneaton or Rugby
for photography or line side observation gave the impression that the
Patriots dominated the top link jobs while the taper boilered 3cyl
engines shared lesser duties with the compounds and the remaining
Claughtons.

We know now, from E. S. Cox, that our impression was not at
fault and the new 5XP class engines were giving serious trouble to
all those concerned with their design and operation. Of all the ills
that can afflict the steam locomotive the inability to steam is the one
beyond all hope of grace. It makes the lives of footplatemen a
nightmare. A series of test runs with the dynamometer car were
run between Euston and Birmingham in competition with the
Patriots and some of the fast runs detailed in Chapter 3 were made
by the older engines. In the *Railway Magazine* for December 1934
Cecil J. Allen described a run by the Stanier 3cyl engine No 5556

which reached the same standard of excellence but the general out-come of the trials was to establish the fact that the new engines, even in test condition, were barely the equal of the older ones and they were definitely less reliable in ordinary everyday service. Early in 1935 there was a general posting of Patriot class engines from the Midland to the LNWR to ensure reliable running on the top link duties while they were replaced on the Midland by 3cyl Stanier engines which took over the Midland workings on the same schedules that the compounds had worked for many years. There were some very disgruntled men on the Midland and hopes for a general acceleration had to be deferred.

It was greatly to the credit of Stanier that no time was wasted on vain regrets or attempts to indulge in wishful thinking but everyone was set to work with energy to cure the trouble. Engines began to appear with slightly different chimneys and wild rumours began to sweep through the LMS. It was noised abroad that half of the LMS kingdom awaited the man who could make the Jubilees steam. As so often happened rumour lagged behind fact and each story gathered a more sensational quality as it passed from mouth to mouth. The Johnnie Knowalls who haunted platform ends throughout the steam era had a glorious field day with such stories as "Stanier has got the sack", "The next batch of 5XPs will be 'Baby Scots' " and "The LMS admit that they should have picked a Gresley man not one from that place in Wiltshire". By the time these rumours reached their height the men behind the scenes had got well on the way to finding the solution to the problem of making the Jubilees steam.

Before a problem can be solved it has to be established why there is a problem at all. There was no single design feature in the Jubilee class that, in itself, made disaster inevitable, it was the combination of a number of unfavourable features which caused so much trouble. The greatest fault was the 14 element superheater which caused a reduction in steam temperature at working pressure of nearly 100deg F as compared with the Patriots. On the face of it this seems to have been a complete loss but, in 1934, there were engines on the GWR which were performing work as good as any in the land with steam at no higher a temperature. A King with low superheat had worked a 575-ton train from Exeter to Paddington 173·5 miles in 175min net; in 1934 such a run had never been surpassed in this country although it had been equalled by a Gresley A3 class Pacific which had run from Kings Cross to York, 188·2 miles, in 192min net with the same load. GWR Castle class engines, with low superheat, had made a number of fast runs on the "Cheltenham Flyer" culminating in a time of 56min 47sec for the 77·3 miles from Swindon to Paddington. It was soon however, made abundantly clear that the conditions which made possible the rock firm steaming of GWR engines on top link service in those days were not to be expected in everyday service on the LMS. With a falling boiler pressure the steam on a Jubilee was often little better than saturated hence the driver's description of "hot water engines".

Among the reasons why the Jubilees could not keep their pressures up to a satisfactory level was the low percentage of free gas area through the tubes expressed in relation to grate area, this amounted to 13per cent against a desirable 15per cent. It might be argued that this was not all that critical a figure because the Peppercorn A1 class Pacifics had a lower percentage and yet they were regarded as good steaming engines. The difference lay in the fact that the A1s were fitted with a correctly proportioned Kylchap double blastpipe and chimney and they were normally worked on tasks well below the potential capacity of a Pacific with a 50ft grate. The Peppercorn A2 class Pacifics which retained their single chimneys had a reputation for erratic steaming. The Jubilees, especially on the Birmingham test trains, were worked closer to their maximum capacity than these Pacifics. The smokebox and blastpipe proportions were based on Swindon practice which worked very well on 2cyl or 4cyl engines. It was claimed later that these dimensions were not suitable for 3cyl engines and some support for this is given by the fact that the 2cyl Stanier mixed traffic 4–6–0s were more successful even in their original low superheated condition. The jumper blastpipe top was an irrelevance because its function was to lessen the blastpipe pressure when working hard; the Jubilee problem was getting enough blastpipe pressure.

The cure for these ills had to be sought by trial and error but perhaps the problem added weight to the case for a national locomotive testing station. The superheater was made larger, the number of elements was increased from 14 to 21 and more space was allowed through the tubes raising the free gas area to 15per cent. This improved the steaming at the expense of efficiency because the smokebox temperature was too high. A larger number of smaller tubes were then used and a further increase to 24 elements was made to the superheater. The blastpipe diameter was reduced to 4⅞in from the original 5¼in. These last modifications raised the engines' ability to steam to an acceptable level and the desired accelerations in service could be allowed to proceed. Later engines had a slightly longer firebox with a grate area of 31sq ft against the original 29·5 sq

The up "Lakes Express" passing Bushey on August 10, 1935 headed by No 5553 with small tender and 5605 with large tender.
[E. R. Wethersett

SOME EARLY DUTIES ON THE LNWR MAIN LINE

No 5652 on a down Euston-Leicester excursion train, via Northampton and Market Harborough, near Carpenders Park.
[E. R. Wethersett

No 5552 *Silver Jubilee* in special
livery at Nottingham Midland during
its tour of the system in 1935.
[T. G. Hepburn

Silver Jubilee heading the up
"Thames-Forth Express" near
Edwalton. The high finish of the
chromium plated steam pipe has
caused "flaring", this same problem
faced earlier photographers of the
Johnson singles with their polished
brasswork.   *[T. G. Hepburn*

SILVER JUBILEE

No 5643 at Kentish Town shed
during indicating trials.
[T. G. Hepburn

No 5684 *Jutland* as fitted with
Kylchap double blastpipe and
chimney 1936-8. [British Railways

No 5553 standing pilot at Rugby.
This engine has been fitted with
a domed boiler and shorter chimney
and has a tender originally intended
for a Patriot class engine. [T. G. Hepburn

TESTS AND
MODIFICATIONS

No 5705 *Seahorse* assisting Royal Scot No 6142 on the down 10.30am
Liverpool express near Bushey.

[E. R. Wethersett]

ft. The steam dome appeared and the top feed clacks were mounted forward of the dome. These modifications cost money and welcome as they were to the footplate staff they were not glad tidings to the accountants. It took time before the improvements spread to all of the class and some were better than others. The later examples could of course be made right from the very start but even the best of them had their occasional lapses when they would not steam but this was a quality shared with many engines that never had to face the same criticism.

The Jubilees never quite overcame the bad initial impression gained in the early months. This was perhaps rather unfair as there were many classes of engine, less in the limelight, that managed to keep their shortcomings well out of sight to all but their enginemen. The general standard of Jubilee performance was compared with the best efforts of top link Patriots in the hands of dedicated crews. The excellent runs of the Patriots detailed in Chapter 3 were not typical of the class over the whole of its existence. The Stanier 2cyl. Black Fives were a success from the start although they also were improved by larger superheaters and domed boilers. There was undue surprise when their 6ft wheels proved capable of high speeds. The ability of small wheeled engines to run fast should never have been in any doubt because even before the 20th Century had dawned the smaller wheeled Jumbos had proved that the real question was not the actual speed but the cost of maintenance at high rotational speeds.

The steam locomotive was an elastic machine and, even in times of adversity, a ruthless driver and a hard working fireman could extract work which was far above the normal standard for the class. In the 1934 test runs with Patriots and Stanier engines No 5556 hauling 345 tons ran from Euston to Blisworth 62·8 miles in 56min 23sec start to stop. Tring Summit was passed at 66mph in the excellent time of 31min 40sec after an unbanked ascent of Camden Bank. If only this standard of running could have been maintained in everyday service there would have been no thoughts of failure attached to the engines. No figures for coal consumption on this run were issued. In the November 1934 *Railway Magazine* Cecil J. Allen described a run on the down "Lakes Express" with No 5552 hauling 415 tons. Tring was passed in 33min 44sec. Again had such timings been consistent the criticism would have been stilled but before we become too overcome by admiration it must be recalled that before World War I George the Fifth class 4–4–0 No 1733 *Grouse* hauling the same 415 ton load, passed Tring in 36min 45sec.

c

Old timers, who remembered the old LNWR in the fullness of its pride were perhaps not unduly impressed by the LMS 4–6–0s.

The closing months of 1934 and the early part of 1935 marked the depth of LMS depression over the Stanier engines. In mid-1935 the first real promise of better things to come was given by the test runs of Pacific No 6200 *The Princess Royal* which brought a 475-ton train up from Crewe to Willesden 152·7 miles in 129min 33sec, this was at least the equal of anything recorded up till then by a GWR King or Gresley Pacific and it was revealed that No 6200 now had an enlarged superheater. There were hopes that similar modifications would help other designs. Although the Jubilee design had not reached its full development No 5552 *Silver Jubilee*, originally No 5642, worked a Motor Dealers' special from Coventry up to Euston in 83min net for the 94 miles. The load was 345 tons and Tring was passed at 63mph and a maximum 88mph was attained downhill. If the aim had been to seek the limelight the LMS could hardly have chosen a worse day because on the same afternoon, September 27, 1935, the new LNER "Silver Jubilee" express made its famous trial run when *Silver Link* averaged 100mph for 43 miles. Against this an ordinary good run could hardly hope to compete and the fact that the LMS engine had the same name as the LNER train caused confusion in some newpapers. A few days later *Silver Jubilee* worked some of the first 1hr 55min services to and from Birmingham, this was most appropriate as 33 years earlier the Webb 4cyl Jubilee class compounds had worked some of the first 2hr services from Euston.

No account of the early years of the Jubilee class would be complete without some mention of an occasion when Patriot and Jubilee combined to make one of the fastest steam runs ever recorded over the Crewe to Willesden main line. The up "Liverpool Flyer" loaded to 12 bogies behind the brand new Jubilee No 5673 still un-named and belonging to the intermediate batch which had the longer firebox and three row superheater but with three rows of seven elements not the three rows of eight elements and modified tubes and flues which came from No 5702 onwards. In front the "Baby Scot" class engine No 5524 *Sir Frederick Harrison* was there to share the work. Fortunately O. S. Nock was on board and he published a brief account of the run in the June 1941 issue of *Railways* and a full log in the April 1966 *Railway Magazine*. The upshot was that the fast time was improved on with three intermediate signal stops and two slight checks; this was equivalent to an unchecked run in 126½min for the 152·7 miles or a start to stop average of 72½mph. Uphill the engines maintained 76–79mph up the rising grades from Nuneaton to Bulkington and Tring Summit was cleared at 75mph while down-hill, 90mph was reached at Castlethorpe and Kenton, 99 miles of this journey had been run at an average of 80mph. The 415-ton load represented 207 tons per engine and size for size the running was equivalent to the daily running of the LNER streamliners.

On the Midland the Jubilees shared the work with the compounds and the new Black Fives as the Patriots had been returned to the LNWR. At first the Jubilees were rarely faster than the compounds on the up grades but quite early it was apparent that the new engines were much faster on the favourable grades. In 1935 Cecil J. Allen was able to report a run on which the 19·6 miles from Luton to Bedford were run in 14 min 35sec with speed varying between 88 and 90mph for a considerable distance. As steaming troubles were overcome the uphill work also improved and, in 1936, Cecil J. Allen was able to publish two runs with loads of 255 and 285 tons respectively and net times of 96½ and 95½min for the 99 miles from Leicester to St Pancras. Such running was not however typical and Cecil J. Allen emphasised that the 4–6–0 mixed traffic engines had, up till then, proved to be more reliable in performance. Gradually the work of the 3cyl engines became more consistent. On other sections in England and Scotland the same story was told but, as 1936 ran its course, the Jubilee reputation began to improve. There was further competition with the Gresley B17 class 4–6–0s on the rival GCR. These engines, in 1936, were allocated to Leicester shed and their work on jobs such as the famous 6.20pm down from Marylebone was a challenge to anything performed on the Midland. The GCR route was not so badly infested with signal delays and their punctuality record was often better. The year 1936 had been a great one for supporters of Gresley and the LNER. The GWR seemed content to bask in the afterglow of former glories and only the stout work of the Princesses on the down "Midday Scot" was anything of a challenge to Doncaster ascendency. In 1937, however, the LMS was destined to make an effective reply.

CHAPTER SIX

Some significant test running

THE YEAR 1937 was a great one for the LMS. It was in 1937 that the
"Coronation Scot" was launched with its spectacular demonstration
run from Euston to Crewe and back. The idea of the super express
such as the "Coronation Scot" was, however, alien to the general
lines of LMS thinking. The LMS had to introduce the "Coronation
Scot" to match the prestige gained by the LNER streamliners, a
true LMS philosophy called for a broad advance in standards on
all routes and for that reason the various test runs carried out with
Class 5 and Class 5X engines were probably more significant for the
LMS than the more spectacular running of the "Coronation Scot".

The Birmingham services were a most important feature of the
express train running on the lines of the former LNWR. These
trains had faced considerable competition from the GWR and in
the 1930s they were suffering from road competition. The LNWR
had been very proud of its Birmingham trains and they were important
from the prestige angle. In the mid-1920s the Georges, which had
done such good service, were replaced by Midland compounds. This
had been an act of poor industrial psychology because the engine-
men were incensed and for a time the running of the compounds
left much to be desired. In the early 1930s however the worst was
over and the men had the measure of the compounds and some
excellent runs were recorded. The best efforts of the Georges however
remained unsurpassed even if they were closely approached. In the
late 1930s the LMS moved with much greater caution in replacing
the Patriots on the Birmingham services by the newer Jubilees.

The LMS ran many tests with the dynamometer car between Euston
and Wolverhampton with 5X class engines of both the parallel
boilered Patriot class and the taper boilered Jubilee class. As indicated
in the previous chapter the trial runs of 1934 had confirmed the
poor initial reputation of the Jubilee class. In general the taper
boilered engines were able to time their test trains but they had no
advantage over the parallel boilered variety in running times and
their work involved higher coal consumption both in terms of lb/mile
and in lb/dbhp/hr. Some of the timekeeping runs had been difficult

36

on the footplate although things may have seemed satisfactory to the passenger in the train. The parallel boilered engines steamed well on the test runs although there was one occasion when leaking joints in the smokebox caused such loss of steam that a pilot engine had to be added at Rugby. This test run was ignored but it proved to be significant in view of the troubles which became common with the built up smokebox engines after World War II.

The test running continued in 1935 and 1936 with various modifications to the taper boilered engines; these included different blastpipe sizes and later different arrangements of superheater tubes. There was also the desire to accelerate the Birmingham trains and the lesson of the trial running was that there was little margin for sensational improvement with either class of 5X engine. Some Birmingham trains were given timings of 1hr 55min instead of the traditional 2hr and one up train was given three stops in the two hour overall booking. These changes came with the introduction of the winter timetable of 1935.

In March and April of 1937 a series of test runs took place on the former LNWR with engine No 5740 *Munster*, one of the final batch of Jubilees with the larger firegrate, the 24 element superheater and with the blastpipe diameter reduced to 4¾in. In March tests were made between Crewe and Carlisle and in April the engine, working from Bushbury shed, ran a series of runs with the dynamometer car between Wolverhampton and Euston. The average load in the up direction was 355 tons and a slightly lower figure of 334 tons was the average in the down direction. Schedules called for running times of 113min up and 116min down and time was kept without difficulty.

The original type of taper boilered engine with low superheat needed over 4lb of coal/dbhp/hr as compared with just over 3·5lb/dbhp/hr with the parallel boilered engines. The intermediate modifications, which included changes in the blastpipe diameter and 21 element superheaters, reduced coal/dbhp/hr figures to within the 3·5 to 4lb range. The tests of 5740 brought this down to the excellent figure of 3·16lb/dbhp/hr. The final modifications had reduced the coal consumption by 30per cent as compared with the original version of the class and by 10per cent as compared with the best results obtained by the Patriot class engines on the same trains in 1935. The Euston–Birmingham road was not difficult but the trains were fast and, under the circumstances the figure of 3·16lb/dbhp/hr was an excellent one. Among the best contemporary 4–6–0s even a GWR Castle could hardly be expected to have shown any significant improvement.

In April 1937 a series of tests was also made between St Pancras and Leeds using a Class 5XP engine and between St Pancras and Manchester using a Class 5 mixed traffic engine. In 1937 the Class 5X engines were not allowed to run between Derby and Manchester. Although outside the scope of this book the running of the mixed traffic engine on the high speed section south of Leicester was very encouraging. The Class 5 engine ran well and attracted most public attention while the Jubilee, perhaps still affected by the poor early reputation of the class, was largely ignored but when the results were published it was shown that the Class 5XP engine had also run very well.

The engine chosen for the Leeds tests was Jubilee No 5614 *Leeward Islands* hauling a test load of 302 tons tare, 305 tons full. The first run was made via Nottingham and an experimental booking of 118½min was set against the fastest contemporary timing of 129min. The timetable compilers had shown considerable skill in estimating the possibilities. Driver Howard and Fireman Hall of Kentish Town shed kept time without difficulty and without any exceptional downhill speeds. The uphill work was excellent and new standards for the Midland main line were foreshadowed. The 4½ miles of 1 in 176 to Sandridge were stormed at a minimum speed of 61mph and the 1 in 120 from Sharnbrook to MP 59¾ was cleared at 53½mph while from Manton speed dropped from 64 to 58mph up two miles of 1 in 142. The highest downhill speeds were 85mph at Flitwick and 87mph at Plumtree. The actual start to stop time from St Pancras to Nottingham, including the most attractive but notoriously tricky piece of line from Kettering to Nottingham, was 117min for the 123½ miles.

On the return journey No 5614 was in charge of Driver North and Fireman George of Leeds shed; this capable crew was destined to achieve some even more spectacular running before the year was out but in April they did well enough to convince even the most diehard supporter of the old Midland that progress really had been made in motive power. Out of Sheffield they accelerated to 44mph up the continuous 1 in 100 to Bradway Tunnel but this was excelled by the start from Nottingham when speed was worked up to 64mph up 6 miles of continuous 1 in 200 to Widmerpool. The climb from Bedford to Luton has always been a testing ground for Midland engines and No 5614 established new standards for the course by climbing the first stretch of 1 in 200 at a minimum of 63mph, recovering quickly to 71 on the "breather" past Flitwick and taking the final 6 miles of 1 in 200 at a minimum of 64½mph. The engine could not have been winded by the climb as there was an acceleration to 77mph on passing Luton. This was a tribute to the skill and endurance of Fireman George at this late stage in a run from Leeds. The 19·6 uphill miles Bedford to Luton had taken 16min 52sec and, after a downhill maximum of 85mph at Hendon, St Pancras was reached in 114min 48sec, 113min net, from Nottingham. This beat all known records for the route.

The following day the run to Leeds was repeated via Leicester. Driver Howard improved slightly on his previous performance as far as Kettering with speeds of 63 at Sandridge, 56 at Sharnbrook Summit and a downhill maximum of 90mph on the descent from Luton to Bedford. Then after a speed of 54 mph at Desborough and a severe slack descending Braybrook Bank, where speed would normally have been high, Leicester was reached in 96min or 92min net. On the return journey Driver North made a relatively moderate start to Kibworth but his time of 16min 33sec from Bedford up to Luton slightly improved on his own excellent figure of the previous day. The speed was higher up the first of the two 1 in 200 banks with a minimum speed of 67mph and it was slightly slower up the second stretch with a minimum of 63mph. There was again an acceleration to 77mph through Luton, another tribute to Fireman George. The start to stop time for the 99·1 miles from Leicester to St Pancras was 92min 28sec and the net time was 90½min. Compared with the best contemporary booked time of 105min there was ample scope for acceleration.

When the tests were made the LMS covered its line of possible retreat by issuing a cautious statement to the effect that no large scale accelerations were necessarily foreshadowed but when the winter timetables were published it was seen that the trials had borne fruit in large measure especially south of Leicester and Nottingham. The main lines to London were not the only Midland lines to be considered and on four consecutive days, October 12–15 a further series of tests of an even more strenuous nature was made from Bristol to Glasgow and back. The engine used throughout the 869 miles was Jubilee No 5660 *Rooke* and the load was the same 302/ 305 tons as on the St Pancras-Leeds trials. The tests made great demands on engine and men. *Rooke* was driven hard on all sections of its test journeys with rapid accelerations from rest and vigorous uphill work. There were no attempts at high downhill maxima despite some long tempting descents. The results of these trials, which are of great importance to the Jubilee story, are summarised in the tables overleaf.

RESULTS OF TESTS WITH No 5660 Rooke

October 12 *Driver* E. Gardner, *Fireman* P. R. Hook, Bristol Shed

	Miles	Min	Sec	Max ihp	Max dhp
Bristol-Gloucester	36·9	37	59		
Gloucester-Cheltenham .. .: ..	6·5	9	15		
Cheltenham-Bromsgrove..	31·1	27	24		
Bromsgrove-Birmingham..	14·4	21	40		
Birmingham-Derby..	41·2	39	29		
Derby-Sheffield	36·3	41	37	1880	1170
Sheffield-Leeds	39·5	45	35		

October 13 *Driver* W. North, *Fireman* H. George, Leeds Shed

	Miles	Min	Sec	Max ihp	Max dhp
Leeds-Carlisle	113·0	117	00	1844	1240
Carlisle-Annan	17·6	19	32		
Annan-Dumfries	15·5	16	45		
Dumfries-Kilmarnock	58·0	61	54	1768	1160
Kilmarnock-Glasgow St Enoch	24·4	28	27		

October 14 *Driver* W. North, *Fireman* H. George, Leeds Shed

	Miles	Min	Sec	Max ihp	Max dhp
Glasgow-Kilmarnock	24·4	29	47		
Kilmarnock-Dumfries	58·0	60	11	1825	1232
		58	15net		
Dumfries-Annan	15·5	15	52		
Annan-Carlisle	17·6	19	49		
Carlisle-Leeds	113·0	115	38	1773	1113

October 15 *Driver* E. Gardner, *Fireman* P. R. Hook, Bristol Shed

	Miles	Min	Sec	Max ihp	Max dhp
Leeds-Sheffield	39·5	47	50		
Sheffield-Derby	36·3	40	27	1802	1250
Derby-Birmingham..	41·2	40	11	1883	1208
Birmingham-Blackwell	12·0	15	35		
Blackwell-Cheltenham	33·4	31	36		
Cheltenham-Gloucester	6·5	9	58		
Gloucester-Bristol	36·9	37	51		

The figures for drawbar horse-power are the actual dynamometer car recordings without the correction for grade in which "equivalent" form dhps are more frequently given. The ihps are calculated, the engine was not fitted with indicating apparatus. The usual cut-off positions on the banks was 35–40per cent with full regulator and it is a tribute to the firemen that no trouble was reported in keeping up the boiler pressure.

Coal consumption

	lb/mile	lb/dbhp/hr	lb/sq ft/grate area
Bristol–Leeds	53·7	4·16	96·4
Leeds–Glasgow	42·7	3·93	77·7
Glasgow–Leeds	43·6	3·87	80·2
Leeds–Bristol	51·1	3·81	91·3

Water consumption

	gal/mile	lb/dbhp/hr	Evaporation lb water/lb coal
Bristol–Leeds	33·7	26·1	6·26
Leeds–Glasgow	29·7	27·3	6·94
Glasgow–Leeds	28·8	25·5	6·58
Leeds–Bristol	35·0	26·2	6·86

In some quarters there has been criticism of the relatively high coal/dbhp/hr figures as compared with the figures of 3lb/dbhp/hr recorded by the Royal Scots and Patriots in test running in 1931 over the LNWR main line. Any such comparison is unfairly based because the conditions were completely different. The test runs of 1931 were over an easily graded main line with relatively moderate schedules and the engines would be steamed at close to their optimum rates. On the other hand *Rooke* was flogged almost to its limit, as it was driven hard away from stops and on the banks with cut offs of 35–40per cent with full regulator. If a Jubilee was steamed at a more constant speed at well below its maximum evaporation rate along the gentle ups and downs of the LNWR a very different result could be expected. A fair analogy can be made with the 1955 tests of a GWR King on the "Cornish Riviera Limited". On the down run the engine was steamed at the rate of 26,000lb/hr but on the up journey the steaming rate was raised to an exceptional 29,000lb/hr because of adverse winds. The coal/dbhp/hr figure was raised from a reasonable 3·21 lb on the down journey to 4·0lb on the harder up journey. It may well have been that *Rooke* was worked as near to its limit as was the larger King on a size for size basis and in such a comparision its coal consumption was reasonable.

The test performances must be regarded as the maximum effort possible for a Jubilee in terms of uphill work, while any further improved times could only come from faster running downhill. The relatively poor evaporation rates of 6·26 to 6·86lb of water/lb coal show that the boiler was pressed beyond the rate for economical steaming. Nevertheless the results were most creditable and the performances recorded on the four days remain among the classics of steam performance. This is especially true of the ascent from Carlisle to Ais Gill when the 48·4 miles to the summit were covered in 48min 36sec. This mighty effort took the LMS timetable compilers by surprise as *Rooke* had gained 10½min on their special test schedule. Elsewhere they had anticipated the actual possibilities with remarkable accuracy.

The Leeds-Carlisle road with its magnificent scenery has romantic associations to match the glories of nature. Shortly after the formation of the LMS the hills thundered with the roar of hard driven engines as rival Midland, LNWR and Caledonian engines fought their way up the banks in all out competition. Again the twilight years of steam saw some epic ascents by Duchess and A4 class Pacifics working rail tours organised by the Railway Correspondence and Travel Society. The hardest part of the northbound journey is the "Long Drag" from Settle Junction to Blea Moor and the following table shows the quality of *Rooke's* performance in comparison with some larger and some smaller engines.

Settle Junction to Blea Moor (13·9 miles average grade 1 in 111)

Class	No	Time min	Average speed	edhp	ihp	ihp/engine weight
MR 990 ..	.. 998	22·0	37·9mph	860	1010	17·3
LNWR Prince	.. 388	21·9	38·0mph	900	1070	16·1
Compound	.. 1008	20·75	40·2mph	975	1155	18·75
Jubilee ..	.. 5660	16·33	51·0mph	1375	1675	21·1
A4 ..	..60019	14·4	57·9mph	1850	2320	23·2
Duchess ..	..46247	14·12	59·0mph	1970	2435	23·2

This table shows the superiority of the Jubilee over the Midland engines and the LNWR Prince not only in actual hp as would be expected but also in power per ton of engine weight. It also shows that the Jubilee was performing work that was only marginally inferior size for size to that of the A4 and the Duchess. No better evidence of the quality of *Rooke's* hill climbing could be desired.

The Midland West of England main line has not featured as strongly in the literature of locomotive performance as the lines to London and the following table of comparative performance is of great interest.

Cheltenham to Bromsgrove (31·1 miles)

Class				No	Load tons	Min	Sec	Max speed mph
Johnson Single	..	..	..	128	215	34	21	
MR Class 2 ..	..	..	..	512	245	34	25	68
MR Class 3 ..	..	..	..	761	305	37	50	64
Compound ..	..	..	..	936	310	29	40	73½
Black Five ..	..	..	..	4964	295	27	41	80
Jubilee ..	..	..	..	5660	305	27	24	80½

This table gives significant evidence of the Jubilee's ascendency over the older Midland engines though the single and the compound have no cause for shame in view of their size and age. The quality of the Black Five's running, which took place in normal service without any special incentive, shows that *Rooke's* performance was in no sense unique when compared with another modern engine of contemporary design. This reinforces the conclusion that can be drawn from the Settle-Carlisle running. The Jubilee class, after modification, was deserving of an honourable but not a leading position among its contemporaries.

The standard of running shown by Nos 5740, 5614 and 5660 gave real promise of worthwhile acceleration of services. On the easy grades of the Birmingham route No 5740 was worked close to the optimum rate of steaming and the engine proved to be reasonably economical. Nos 5614 and 5660 were tested over steeper gradients and had to be driven very hard with firing rates of up to 100lb/sq ft of grate area. This was considered to be beyond the range of economical working and beyond the rate of working that could be recommended for regular daily operation. Under the circumstances and remembering that they were associated with maximum efforts, the coal/dbhp/hr figures of 3·93 to 4·13 recorded by 5614 and 3·81 to 4·16lb/dbhp/hr by 5660 were just as creditable as the lower figure of 3·16lb/dbhp/hr of 5740 on the easier grades of the Birmingham line. The maximum calculated ihp figures of over 1800ihp were very high for an engine of this size but they could hardly be expected to be sustained in steady steaming conditions. It must also be remembered that the engines were not actually indicated but the published ihp figures were calculated on the basis of indicator diagrams obtained on other occasions. Postwar test techniques using more sophisticated methods have suggested that many of the earlier ihp figures were over estimated. For this reason it is perhaps safer, for comparative purposes, to accept 1,800 as the maximum ihp rather than the figure of 1,880 claimed for 5660 at several points and the even higher 1,908 claimed at one point for 5614. It remains a valid, fully established, fact that a Jubilee could, under test conditions, stand up to merciless flogging and reached a very high ihp.

It emerged from the trials that a well handled Jubilee could be expected to take a load of 300 tons up 1 in 100 at a sustained 45mph, up 1 in 200 at over 60mph and up 1 in 300 at 67mph or over. This meant that Sharnbrook and Desborough summits could be passed at over 50mph in either direction. The same 300-ton load could be expected to be hauled at 80mph on the level and at 90mph downhill. In 1937 the whole class of 191 engines was in service with a growing reputation far better than that during the "winter of discontent" of 1934/5 when the low superheat engines were "working hydraulic" to the infinite grief of their crews. The final modifications which brought about this happier state of affairs had not spread to all of the class but even those engines which still retained their 14 element superheaters had blastpipe modifications which made them far better than the originals. There were still some difficult trips but, at their best, those with the 24 element superheaters such as 5740, 5614 and 5660 compared reasonably well with contemporary 4–6–0s of similar size on the LMS and on other railways. The LMS had spent considerable sums of money on new locomotives and they were, in 1937, at last able to expect some return on their capital.

CHAPTER SEVEN

Improved daily running

THE WINTER SCHEDULES of 1937 brought a revolution to express train services over the Midland main line. A whole crop of even time bookings appeared in the timetables and in order to work the new schedules 51 Jubilees were stationed on the Midland. These were reinforced by 49 Class 5 4–6–0 mixed traffic engines. The load for the fastest bookings was fixed at 300 tons for Class 5XP, 255 tons for Class 5 and 220 tons for the compounds. With 100 Stanier 4–6–0s available it was expected that compounds would only be required to work the fastest trains in rare emergencies. The Midland has often been described as a "small engine line" but no engine is large or small except in relation to the job. A Duchess would be a very small engine on the New York Central while a Jubilee was quite a large engine for 300 tons. The secret of working fast trains over a sharply graded road lay in a high power/weight ratio.

The first week of the new timings was a week of autumn fogs and there were a number of delays. It must also be remembered that, in 1937, there was still a good deal of freight traffic and the stopping train had not been abolished; it was not always easy to thread the high speed trains through the other traffic. Nevertheless there were some notable runs recorded even on the first day. The 2pm up from Manchester weighing 300 tons and hauled by the engine No 5694 *Bellerophon* arrived in St Pancras in 97min 33sec from Leicester in spite of a signal stop near Kentish Town. Behind this the up Scottish express, due in at 6.16pm, came storming up through the shires in even better fashion. No 5734 *Meteor* converted a late start from Leicester to an early arrival by covering the 99.1 miles in an actual time of 90min 57sec with 290 tons. This was running, in ordinary service, very close to the standard of *Leeward Islands'* test trip. The start of *Meteor's* run was the hitherto unheard of time of 26min 19sec from Leicester to passing Kettering with a speed of 55mph at Desborough Summit. The up "Thames Forth Express" had a bad road but still covered the 105·3 miles from Melton in 105min including a dead stand for 2min at Whissendine. No 5663 was hauling 2 55 tons. Some of the fast trains had very light loads and some new

44

records were made such as passing Luton in 30min 2sec from St Pancras with 225 tons. The old Midland even in its greatest days had never seen such running as this.

The best running standards represented the bright side of the coin but against this Cecil J. Allen wrote in the *Railway Magazine* that out of 31 recorded runs, 11 were on time or early, 10 were less than a minute over schedule and 10 runs or one-third of the total were late. Signal or permanent way delays accounted for most of the lost time but there were two occasions when time was booked against the engine. Two runs with time booked against the engine out of 31 trips would have been considered very good in postwar Britain but in 1937 something better was expected. The general conclusion was however that if only better paths could have been found the new timetables were a thoroughly practical proposition. The Jubilees were shown to have a reasonably good margin in hand with the 300-ton load. A limit of 300 tons did not leave much margin for attaching extra vehicles and I well remember a journey down to Leicester in 1938 when, with a load of 11 bogies, 385 tons, a Class 2 4-4-0 was taken as pilot. The Jubilee made the veteran run faster than it would ever have done under its own volition. The Luton Bedford section took a few seconds over 14min with a well sustained spell at 90mph but the pair was not unduly vigorous uphill and the time to Leicester was 103min or 98min net. At Leicester the Class 2 pilot came off and the Jubilee continued assisted by a compound.

A few runs of really exceptional merit were published by C. J. Allen in 1938/9. No 5622 *Nyasaland* with a 7-coach load of 235 tons gross made what was perhaps the fastest run ever recorded by steam over the Midland main line. The net time was 84½min for the 99·1 miles from Leicester to St Pancras. The uphill work was excellent with an acceleration from a severe slack to 38mph through Market Harborough to 60mph at Desborough Summit up continuous 1 in 132. After a slack to 57mph through Irchester the minimum at MP 59¾ was 56mph while the two stretches of 1 in 200 between Bedford and Luton were topped at 72 and 71mph. Downhill there were four 90mph maxima and one of 89mph, the highest was 95 mph at Radlett. This standard of running was described by Cecil J. Allen as being of equal merit, weight for weight of engine, to the running of the LNER streamliners. Driver Howard of Kentish Town, who drove No 5614 on some of its test runs, came up from Leicester in a net time of 88min with No 5598 *Basutoland* hauling 275 tons.

The best run in the down direction was made by No 5616 *Malta* with a 10-coach load of 320 tons. Bedford was passed in 44min 8 sec for the 49·8 miles with a minimum speed of 63½min at Sandridge and maxima of 92mph down the two stretches of 1 in 200 between Luton and Bedford. Luton was passed in 30min 6 sec from St Pancras and Driver Senior of Millhouses Shed, Sheffield, did not know he was being timed.

Good as these times and speeds are they are of course commonplace to those familiar with today's standards and in order to put things into perspective it is necessary to tabulate the records of the Jubilees in relation to other steam engines that had run on the Midland prior to 1937.

Leicester to St Pancras (99·1 miles)

Kirtley	..	..	..2–4–0	800 class	210 tons	110min
Johnson	..	..	..4–2–2	7ft 4in Single	150 tons	101½min
Rebuild	..	..	..4–4–0	Class 2 saturated	210 tons	105½min
Rebuild	..	..	..4–4–0	Class 2 superheated	177 tons	103¾min
700	..	..	..4–4–0	Class 3 superheated	202 tons	102¼min
Compound	..	..	..4–4–0	Class 4 superheated	260 tons	99min net
Black Five	..	..	..4–6–0	Class 5, test run	260 tons	91min net
Jubilee	..	..	..4–6–0	Low superheat	285 tons	95min net
Jubilee	..	..	..4–6–0	No 5614, test run	302 tons	89min net
Jubilee	..	..	..4–6–0	No 5598	280 tons	88min net
Jubilee	..	..	..4–6–0	No 5622	235 tons	84½min net

In the down direction the best timing point for comparative purposes is Bedford as it then becomes possible to eliminate the effects of checks and easings.

St Pancras to passing Bedford (49·8 miles)

Johnson	..	..	..4–4–0	*Beatrice*	150 tons	52¾min
Johnson	..	..	..4–2–2	7ft 6in Single	188 tons	53½min
Johnson	..	..	..4–4–0	Class 3 saturated	170 tons	45½min
Johnson	..	..	..4–4–0	Class 3 superheated	245 tons	52¾min
Fowler	..	..	..4–4–0	Standard compound	290 tons	48½min
Fowler	..	..	..4–6–0	Patriot	345 tons	49min
Stanier	..	..	..4–6–0	Jubilee	320 tons	44½min

The above selection of runs is taken from the writings of C. Rous Marten, the Rev W. J. Scott, Cecil J. Allen and David L. Smith. Purists may challenge the name Fowler being given to the standard compounds which were the work of Smith, Johnson, Deeley and Fowler but the final form appeared under Fowler and it was under Fowler that the engines were superheated. A run of almost equal merit to the above run by a standard compound, which was published in the *SLS Journal* in an article by D. L. Smith, was published by Cecil J. Allen in the *Railway Magazine*. The most famous performer among the Midland compounds, No 1008, with the same 290-ton load, passed Bedford in 50min

5sec. The run by the Johnson Belpaire 4–4–0 in its original form was timed by C. Rous Marten when he was making a special test of the highly competitive schedule of 3hr 35min introduced in 1904. The engine was No 2788 driven by Driver Selly who had given Mr Rous Marten several outstanding runs. In 1937 the 3hr 35min schedule was reintroduced with more intermediate stops.

The improved standards of running on the Midland enhanced the line's reputation in the years leading up to 1939 but many Leicester and Nottingham residents remained faithful to the GCR. The GC main line was less crowded by trains and better paths were given to the expresses. In 1937 the Class B17 4–6–0s, despite their reputation for bad riding, were running very well. The work that the Leicester GC drivers were performing on the 8.51am up and the 6.20pm down from Marylebone compared favourably with the best daily work of the Jubilees.

On the LNWR main line the heaviest duties were performed by the Pacifics and the Royal Scots. The Patriots continued to be used on many of the faster light trains right up to World War II. This was especially true of the Birmingham trains. The 65mph booking from Rugby to Watford was inaugurated by Jubilees but afterwards Patriots were mainly concerned. They performed this duty with conspicuous success especially when D. S. Barrie timed No 5525 over the 65·1miles in 59min 6sec with 390 tons. In mid-March 1939 there was a general posting of Jubilees to the sheds of Bushbury and Aston with a view to their replacing the Patriots on the fast Birmingham jobs. In the autumn of 1938 I remember asking a member of the Derby CME's department which was the better engine, the Patriot or the Jubilee? He gave a reply which showed his clear conviction that the superior mechanical design of the Jubilee would inevitably establish its superiority for everybody to see. It seemed as if the March transfers were a confirmation of this but the eclipse of the Patriots was not complete for in June 1939 the *Railway Observer* reported a fast run by a Patriot on the 65mph booking.

There was some experimental running on the Birmingham services by engine No 5684 *Jutland* which was fitted with a Kylchap double blastpipe and chimney. This was not a success on this engine as it threw fire in such a way as to suggest that the engine was trying to reinact the famous naval battle after which it was named. A run by this engine was described by Cecil J. Allen in the September 1938 *Railway Magazine*. The 62·8 miles from Euston to Blisworth were covered in 61min 59sec with a load of 365 tons, an adequate performance but one which would not have been exceptional for one of the standard single chimneyed engines. E. S. Cox in *Chronicles of Steam* (Ian Allan 1967) explains how the lesson was learnt that the exhaust arrangements had to be suitable for the type and size of the boiler. In this country the Kylchap exhaust, as opposed to the simple double blastpipe, gave its best results on the larger boilers of the LNER Pacifics.

One of the best runs ever recorded by a Jubilee on the former LNWR main line took place when No 5558 *Manitoba*, driven by the redoubtable Laurie Earl, headed the Edinburgh portion of the up "Royal Scot" with 290 tons from Carlisle to Euston. The net time for the 299·1 miles was 279min or 4min inside the schedule of the 310–ton "Coronation Scot" with its Pacific. The net time for the 158·1 miles from passing Crewe to Euston was 140min and from Rugby it was 71min for 82·6 miles. The hill climbing was of outstanding quality throughout; up the 7 miles of 1 in 125 from Clifton speed fell from 55 to 51½mph and 59mph was steadily maintained up the 1 in 177 of Madeley Bank. A speed of 76 to 80mph was maintained up gently rising grades between Bletchley and Cheddington and 82mph was reached on the gradual descent from Garstang to Brock.

In conditions of heavier loading, O. S. Nock in his book *William Stanier* (Ian Allan 1964) describes an emergency substitution of No 5592 for a Royal Scot on the up "Midday Scot" with a load of 505 tons. After a very laboured start up Madeley Bank No 5592 ran reasonably well covering the 158·1 miles in 171½min, a loss of 6min on schedule. No 5592 was then in original condition with two row superheater; doubtless a better performance would have been recorded with an engine with the later modifications. An example of Jubliee performance over Shap Summit with a fairly substantial load, was described by O. S. Nock in the *Railway Magazine*. Engine No 5696 *Arethusa* with a load of 445 tons, timed by A. Mellor, covered the 90·1 miles from Preston to Carlisle in a net time of 96½min. The famous climb from Carnforth to Shap Summit 31·4 miles took 40min 45sec which compares in interesting fashion with a run timed by the late Maj H. Myers in the heyday of the Claughtons when a time of 42min 39sec was made by *Sir Gilbert Claughton* with 440 tons.

On the Caledonian main line No 5636 *Uganda* passed Beattock Summit 49·7 miles from the Carlisle start in 50min 3sec equalling the schedule of the "Coronation Scot" though with 245 tons against the 310 tons for the Pacifics. Over the sharply undulating Perth–Aberdeen main line one of the most outstanding performers was No 5727 *Inflexible*. Cecil J. Allen described runs by this engine, with loads of

No 45711 *Courageous* passing
Monkton with the 4.20pm Stranraer-
Glasgow train in September 1954.
[W. J. V. Anderson

**THE STRANRAER
ROAD**

SOME DULL AND DIRTY JUBILEES

Top: No 45739 in wartime black photographed at Kingmoor. The figure 4 has been added in smaller lettering.   *[T. G. Hepburn*

Centre: No 45634 *Trinidad* at Crewe North shed in 1952 still in LMS livery.   *[J. F. Clay*

Below: No 45597 *Barbados* on up Sheffield express near Aylestone Junction in 1951. The engine is fitted with a parallel sided BR pattern chimney and has a Royal Scot tender. It was too dirty to identify its intended livery.   *[J. F. Clay*

SOME JUBILEE LIVERIES

Top: No 45565 *Victoria* in special light green experimental livery heads a St Pancras-Leeds express, with coaches in "Plum and spilt milk", past Upper Broughton at very high speed.   *[T. G. Hepburn*

Above: No 45700 *Amethyst* in LNWR style livery.   *[British Railways*

Below: No 45682 *Trafalgar* in GWR type Brunswick green finally chosen for BR express engines. Photographed at Crewe North.   *[T. G. Hepburn*

CLIMBING BEATTOCK

Jubilee No 45738 *Samson* climbing Beattock Bank with a heavy north-bound train in August 1963. *[W. J. V. Anderson*

275 tons, covering the 73·7 miles from Perth to Stonehaven in 72min 57sec and returning in 72min 45sec.

The possibilities of the Jubilee class on the G&SWR "Long Road" from Glasgow to Carlisle were shown by the trial running of *Rooke* but an interesting working was introduced on the Glasgow St Enoch to Ayr route where the traditional 50min timing of the old Sou'West was reduced to 45min. The 41·3 mostly level miles were frequently run in even time by Jubilee class engines with loads just over or under 300 tons. These Jubilees were engines from Patricroft shed Manchester filling in a gap in their rosters before returning to their home shed by running to Ayr and back. They were in the hands of Polmadie drivers and they performed much faster running than the admittedly smaller engines of the former G&SWR or the standard compounds or Class 2 4–4–0s which had formerly run on this route. This was an example of the fulfillment of the aim of replacing older engines by a modern design capable of faster running and greater daily mileage.

On the L&Y much the same story can be told. Jubilee class engines used on the former LNWR route from Liverpool to Manchester showed their ability to run at up to 80mph on the level with loads of 300 tons but equally good times were recorded by the Patriots and enlarged Claughtons. The pride of the old L&Y had been the "Blackpool Club Train" which had traditionally been the job for a specially tuned and cleaned Aspinall Atlantic or Hughes 4–6–0. It became the job for a 5XP, Jubilee or Patriot, which had worked a train from Glasgow to Manchester earlier in the same day.

All in all during the years 1937/9 the Jubilees were fulfilling the aims of their designer and were proving to be worthy members of the Stanier family. The high performance standards shown in the 1937 trials were shown to be possible on occasions in ordinary daily service. The engines were working long daily rosters and their general standard of running was high. There were however occasional lapses which made the footplate men concerned over the relatively small margins to meet adverse operating conditions. The engines were new and the coal was usually of good quality. It also has to be remembered that the final two years up the World War II were years of very high standards of steam engine running on all British railways. The performances of the Jubilees were closely matched by the Patriots and the Black Fives on the LMS, by the B17s on the LNER, by the Stars and Castles on the GWR and the Southern enthusiasts could point out that these 4–6–0s were closely approached by their 4–4–0s of the Schools class.

D

The year 1939 was one of great promise for the LMS; there had been the test runs of the Pacific No 6234 *Duchess of Abercorn* which showed the great potential power of the Duchess class, there were hints of engines on the drawing board which would have meant a further advance in standards, the various smaller standard engines, including the Jubilees, were doing well, the autumn timetables, which never came into operation, promised a further step towards the general acceleration of LMS services but all these hopes vanished in the world catastrophe of September 1939.

CHAPTER EIGHT

A rough war

IN THE FIRST emergency timetable of October 1939 all the progress in train speeds, so slowly made at first but later coming as a dramatic advance, all vanished at a stroke. In World War I the first two years saw little or no deterioration in speeds; in fact 1915 was a vintage year for LNWR performance and the slow schedules only came into operation gradually. In World War II the worst possible happenings were expected from the very start and it was thought that train services would be disrupted by bombing. A basic timetable was put into operation at once and this proved to be unduly cautious during the period of "phoney war" in the winter of 1939. A rather better timetable was introduced in December 1939 and this timetable continued to be the basic pattern, though of course subject to considerable modification, throughout the war. The original time-tables presupposed a maximum speed limit to 60mph and start to stop bookings to 45mph. In December some bookings were allowed to reach 50mph start to stop and throughout the war a rather blind eye was turned on maximum speeds in some areas. The wartime bookings were however a sad falling in standards from the host of 60mph timings and frequent 90mph maxima attained during the years immediately leading up to the outbreak of war. The tragedy of the ruination of train services was of course overshadowed by the major tragedy of war.

The working of wartime trains resembled the running of peace-time fitted freight services, loads being very heavy but speeds were low and stops more frequent. This was especially true of the Midland section of the LMS where every train became a semi-fast. The sure footed nature of 4-6-0 locomotives allowed the Jubilees to make their initial starts without slipping but they had neither the boiler nor cylinder power to accelerate very quickly with loads up to 50per cent heavier than those for which they had been intended. There was not much in reserve to meet the poor quality coal that became the staple diet of all railways as the war progressed. As call up proceeded it was difficult for the railways to retain enough skilled men for locomotive maintenance and those that did remain each had to do the work of several men in increasingly difficult conditions. In the first half of the war however the Jubilees managed reasonably well. In November 1939 the *Railway Magazine* reported that a well known Camden driver had run the 1.10pm from Euston to Crewe in scheduled time despite a load of 537 tons tare, 580 tons full with Jubilee class engine No 5624. This was a good effort under the circumstances but it did not exceed in merit the many occasions when LNWR Georges and Princes had worked trains of 480–500 tons on similar bookings during the final months of 1918.

In September 1942 a correspondent wrote to Cecil J. Allen expressing his admiration for the work of the Jubilee class since they had received the larger superheaters. He claimed that the work he had seen performed on the Midland, such as climbing Desborough Bank with 16 bogies and frequently with 14 or 15, was as good, size for size, as anything recorded with the Pacifics. In common with other servicemen of my generation I made many journeys behind Jubilee class engines on the Midland main line north and south of Leicester and over the Midland West of England main line. Loads were usually 12–14 bogies and nothing spectacular was ever expected and never happened but there was no case of the engine not being up to the job. Most of these journeys were undertaken in the cause of leave, granted, wangled or taken and in no case did a Jubilee land me in trouble by late running. In the later years of the war I was posted to areas that involved travel on other lines and doubtless the Jubilees deteriorated with the rest.

Cecil J. Allen gave some more specific details of Jubilee performance in wartime in the September 1942 *Railway Magazine*. The specially finished No 5552 *Silver Jubilee* was reputed to be a consistant performer on the 2.15pm from Manchester to Euston via Stoke. The time from Stoke to Rugby was 76min 14sec despite a load of 475 tons and a signal check near Colwich. The *Railway Observer* reported the arrival of the 6pm Up Wolverhampton express 13min early at Euston which meant that No 5556 *Nova Scotia* had brought a 465-ton train up from Coventry 94 miles in 102min. A much more spectacular and unusual performance for wartime took place on the Midland main line when No 5594 *Bhopal* with a very light load for wartime of 270 tons ran up from Kettering to St Pancras 72 miles in 73min 35sec or 69min net equalling the prewar XL timing. It was a gain of 26min on the wartime schedule. Runs of this quality sometimes happened in wartime, occasionally the presence of a VIP on the train was the reason.

The biggest fall in running standards took place on the high speed main lines. Over heavily graded routes, where downhill speeds were restricted, the wartime restrictions made less difference. North of Leeds and over the former G&SWR the demand made on the engines was little less than prewar. In the early part of the war a run was made by No 5566 *Queensland* with a load of 430 tons. Blea Moor was passed in 28min 26sec from the Hellifield start against a timetable allowance of 33min. The run was timed by G. J. Aston but when giving the details in November 1944 Cecil J. Allen pointed out that by then the standards of Jubilee class running over this route had deteriorated considerably.

In the autumn of 1942 Cecil J. Allen had timed an excellent run southbound over the G&SWR main line. The engine No 5594 *Bhopal* with 405 tons covered the 58·1 miles from Kilmarnock to Dumfries in 65min 29sec. This was work close to the best peacetime standards but there had been downhill speeds in excess of the wartime limits including some 80mph maxima. By 1944 however the declining condition of many of the engines coupled with the poor coal caused a sad falling off from earlier standards on many occasions. On two successive runs Mr Allen had seen Jubilee class engines stall for want of steam, once at Ribblehead and once at Blea Moor while on the Caledonian main line he had seen speed fall to 20mph on the 1 in 200 beyond Gretna. He also recorded a journey northwards on the LNWR main line with the 8.30am ex-Euston where a Jubilee was asked to haul a crowded 16 coach train and a fierce side wind caused the engine to lose 10min to Stafford. For work such as this a more powerful design would have been desirable.

Shortly before the outbreak of war there had been rumours that a 4cyl version of the Jubilee class was being planned but E. S. Cox in *Locomotive Panorama Vol 1* makes it clear that in actual fact thoughts had been turning towards a two cylinder 5XP. The loss of the inside cylinder and motion would allow a larger 250lb boiler to be used but in due course civil engineering restrictions allowed the larger boiler to be used on the three cylindered engine. The new boiler was a shortened version of that used on No 6170 *British Legion*, the rebuild of the ill-fated high pressure engine *Fury*. A double blastpipe and chimney was fitted. This was of the simple double blastpipe pattern as used on the Duchess class following the successful trial running of No 6234 *Duchess of Abercorn* in 1939. The Kylchap had been removed from *Jutland* before the war and experiments had been made with the simpler apparatus on another Jubilee class engine. There were also small but valuable modifications to cylinder and valve design on the rebuilt Jubilees. The engines selected for rebuilding were No 5735 *Comet* and No 5736 *Phoenix* and they were at first allocated to Leeds for working the difficult road to Glasgow St Enoch. The success of these engines led to the large scale conversion to taper boiler of the Royal Scot class.

In the January 1944 *Railway Magazine* Cecil J. Allen described some runs by the rebuilt Jubilee and Royal Scot class engines which were a tonic against the generally depressing contemporary background. In the northbound direction No 5736 *Phoenix* with a load of 430 tons ran from Dumfries to Kilmarnock 58 miles in a net time of 61min a clear gain of 7min on the exceptionally good run for a standard Jubilee timed in 1942 despite an extra 25 tons. Southbound the late R. E. Charlewood timed sister engine No 5735 *Comet* with a 410-ton train with no assistance through the Barrhead Gap. The 1 in 70 bank was taken comfortably at a minimum speed of 32mph and Kilmarnock was reached in 29½min net against a schedule of 34min. The 58 miles from Kilmarnock to Dumfries were covered in 62½min or 61½min net a fitting counterpart to the run by the same class of engine in the northbound direction. The good running continued over the short sections to Carlisle. Side by side Cecil J. Allen described running of the same high standard by the rebuilt Royal Scot class engines.

The Royal Scots retained their 18in cylinders on rebuilding and the converted Jubilees their 17in cylinders while both classes kept their 9in diameter valves. In later postwar years, when faster running was possible, some drivers claimed that the engines with 17in cylinders and the larger valve/cylinder ratio were the freer running. There was little noticeable difference in recorded timings. At first the rebuilt Jubilees were left in Class 5XP against Class 6 for the Royal Scots with their larger cylinders and nominal tractive effort but after a short time the rebuilt Jubilees were up-rated to Class 6 because of their performances. The limited wartime resources were used where they were most needed and the conversion of the Royal Scot class had first priority. Later a number of Patriots were converted. The Royal Scots and Patriots both suffered to an increasing degree from leakage round the Midland type of built up smokebox and the Great Western type of cylindrical smokebox proved to be better in this respect. No more Jubilees were converted after the initial two but, had nationalisation not taken place, it is probable that the LMS would have converted more Jubilees when the Patriot conversions were complete.

As things were the bulk of the Jubilees had to struggle on unaltered against increasingly adverse conditions as the war dragged out its weary length. An interesting extension of their working was their penetration of the steeply graded line to Stranraer. This section had formerly been worked by mixed traffic engines of the 2–6–0 Crab and the 4–6–0 Black Five classes. Some people seemed surprised that the large wheeled engines could do so well but actually the Jubilees had one big advantage over the Black Five class because of their greater adhesion weight. The value of using the Jubilee class on the Stranraer Road was that maximum mileage rosters could be worked. Some of the Jubilees on this service were Crewe North engines awaiting a return working to their own shed. They were allowed 14 bogies between Glasgow and Ayr, 10 to Girvan and eight to Stranraer. A run with a 14-coach load as far as Ayr was described by Cecil J. Allen in the September 1944 *Railway Magazine*; a net time of 47min was made with 460 tons behind No 5579 *Punjab*. The traditional G&SWR booking had been 50min with lighter loads. As an example of the uphill work on the steepest grades No 5575 *Madras* with 225 tons climbed the notorious bank from New Luce with its famous reverse curve known as the Swan's Neck at a sustained 31–33mph, with no initial impetus this was good work. The Jubilee class engines were allowed heavier maximum loadings over Peak Forest in Derbyshire another concession to their superior adhesion weight.

During the war, freight traffic was of paramount importance and many express engines found themselves on freight duties for most of their time. The Jubilees took their share of wartime freight and for a time in the latter part of the war compounds found themselves again on Birmingham expresses, especially weekend extras, because the 4–6–0s were employed on work of greater national importance. Nevertheless some Jubilees continued to do quite well on express trains right up to the end of hostilities. In the later stages of the war Cecil J. Allen published details of a run with No 5647 *Sturdee* with a 15-coach train of 530 tons full. There was inevitably a very slow start from Euston and there was the fear of catching up a train which was just in front but the net time to Rugby was 98min for the 82·6 miles. Much better running followed; there was the usual very slow start perhaps predictable with a Jubilee and 530 tons but the 36·2 miles from Brinklow to Rugeley were run in 36min 12sec with maxima of 67 at Nuneaton and 68mph at Polesworth. The net time for the 63·3 miles from Rugby to Stoke was 72min.

One of the best runs recorded by a Jubilee class engine in the final wartime months was timed by O. S. Nock from the footplate. O. S. Nock has described this run in detail in a number of books and magazines but it remains a story still worth retelling. A photograph of the train was published in the magazine *Railways* the forerunner of today's *Railway World*, the grimy unrelieved black appearance of the engine did not promise much but the engine showed its ability to come very near in places to the hp output of the test engine *Rooke* in 1937. A pilot was taken from Glasgow to Kilmarnock where the rebuilt engine *Comet* had managed so well on its own but after Kilmarnock the engine No 5565 *Victoria* continued on its own with 410 tons. It needed hard work on the uphill sections to reach Dumfries in a net time of 66min and at one point the cut off was 50per cent with full regulator. Steam pressure was maintained but there was a fall in water level.

Continuing southwards from Carlisle with the 410-ton train *Victoria* ran the 30·8 miles to Appleby in 38min 43sec. This was followed by, perhaps, the best work of the whole journey when Ais Gill was passed in 30min 30sec from the Appleby start. The sustained speed on the long 1 in 100 stretch past Kirkby Stephen was a steady 38mph, with a load of 410 tons this was work of the same quality that took *Rooke* up the same grade at a sustained 46mph with 305 tons. *Victoria* needed 37per cent cut off with full regulator to achieve this result. Boiler pressure and water level remained constant. This was an example of Jubilee wartime working at its best, a strong willing engine that cheerfully accepted hard work. It must have called for skilled and hard firing. At the same time it must be admitted that the rebuilds with the larger boiler performed similar work with greater ease and not every Jubilee run was at this level. The war found the weak spots in the design of many engines and the Jubilees were no exceptions. There were a lot of Jubilees and their activities spread over a wide area. Many people noticed the times when they fell from grace and cursed the class of engine and the railways in general but perhaps, if the full story could be told and due allowance made for the difficulties, it would emerge that the wartime contribution of the Jubilees was the most useful phase of their lives.

CHAPTER NINE

A slow recovery

WHEN PEACE RETURNED in 1945 enthusiasts hoped for a speedy
restoration of prewar speeds but in actual fact the railway industry
never regained its 1939 position in the life of the nation. War had
made the operation of railways much more difficult, fuel was more
expensive and often of poor quality and the wages bill was much
heavier. There had been a great stimulus to the development of the
internal combustion engine during the war, but for the first few years
of peace restrictions on the sale of motor vehicles for the home
market and petrol rationing shielded the railways from the fierce
competition that was to come. The immediate postwar years were
years of disappointment and frustration on the railway. The depth
of depression was reached in the winter of 1947 with its snows and
shortages. Rail travel became as miserable as it had been during the
war but while people had been ready to blame the malice of the
enemy their anger now turned on the railway industry in general
and the dying companies in particular.

Shortly after the end of the war with Japan the LNER announced
a bold programme of acceleration of services and the LMS was
criticised for its greater caution. As events proved the LNER
accelerations were premature and could not be fully sustained but
the LMS moved slowly forward. All over Britain the performance
of steam locomotives was a variable factor of operation, the brightest
spot was the running of the nearly new Bulleid Pacifics and the newly
rebuilt Royal Scots. The Jubilees were in no way superior to a low
general average but there were some bigger and more famous engines
that were no better during the final years of the 1940s.

As with many other classes the Jubilees at times produced flashes
of brilliance well above the general contemporary level. In the
January 1946 *Railway Magazine* Cecil J. Allen published a run by
No 5628 *Somaliland* hauling a 13-coach load on the 1.30pm from
St Pancras. The 19·6 largely falling miles from Luton to Bedford
were run in 21min 8sec start to stop with a maximum speed of
85mph approaching Elstow. Continuing beyond Kettering, still with
its 430-ton load, *Somaliland* passed Oakham, 21·8 miles from the

start, in 26min 32sec, with such a load on such a road this was good running. The following month something of the gloss was taken from the downhill running when Cecil J. Allen timed a Black Five at 92mph before Bedford with a 400-ton train. When news of these high speeds was noted by authority at Derby some locomotive inspectors were summoned into the presence to be told that such enthusiasm must be restrained in future.

Generally speaking the Black Five was preferred to the Jubilee during these first prewar years. The operating department cried out for as many mixed traffic engines as could be built. Until track repairs had been carried out there would be little scope for large numbers of express engines. No further rebuilds of Jubilee class engines took place; work was concentrated on completing the conversion of the Royal Scots and the rebuilding of a number of Patriots. There was however a large number of unaltered Jubilees in service and these had to be used. They did a lot of hard unspectacular work especially on such services as the long through workings between Bristol and York. It would be rare for an enthusiast to record anything spectacular but services of this nature earned money for the railway and provided service to the public. The frequent stops and the hard work needed to pick up speed from colliery slacks and other speed restrictions added to the work required of the engine crews. Generally speaking the Jubilees acquitted themselves well on work of this kind, much of the late running of cross country trains came from causes other than locomotive deficiency.

On the LNWR main line the Jubilees were very much a secondary type of engine with the heaviest trains worked by the Pacifics and the Converted Scots and Patriots. At first the Jubilees retained their position on the Manchester trains routed via Stoke but following nationalisation the standard Britannia class Pacifics took over the hardest duties. The unrebuilt Patriots which retained their original boilers fell to a level of performance sadly lower than their excellent prewar reputation. The main trouble was air leaking through the joints in the built-up type of smokebox, making steaming a problem. The Jubilees had certainly stood the test of time better than their 1934 rivals. It was rare for an express on the LNWR main line to get a good road and the general standard of timekeeping was poor. The locomotives were not always to blame and the frequent signal and pw delays must have taken the heart out of all but the most dedicated of engine crews.

Two typical examples of valuable but unspectacular running on the LNWR main line were recorded by Norman Harvey in 1949. On the 8.55am from Euston to Wolverhampton engine No 45726 *Vindictive* with a load of 14 bogies weighing 470 tons full ran from Euston to Watford 17·4 miles in 24min 45sec against a booking of 25min and from Watford to Blisworth 45·4 miles in 49min 52sec, schedule 50min. The minimum speed at Tring was 53mph and the maximum at Leighton Buzzard was 72mph. This was a good example of exact timekeeping by the Bushbury crew; it was the type of engine-manship which served the railway well but got little publicity. The Birmingham trains were heavier than prewar but they were slower. In February 1950 Cecil J. Allen described some runs from Birmingham to Coventry with 400-ton trains. The Jubilee class engine No 45721 *Impregnable* covered the 18·9 miles from Birmingham to Coventry in 21min 19sec against a booking of 23min. A Rebuilt Patriot class engine with the same load took 20min 37sec.

A rather better run on the Birmingham road was described in the November 1951 issue of *Railways*. O. S. Nock published a run timed by J. C. Keyte with the Jubilee class engine No 45703 *Thunderer*, a name associated with good running on the Birmingham services by the Precursor class engine of the same name. The load was 450 tons and the time from Birmingham to Coventry was 21min 50sec; equal in merit to the preceding run in view of the heavier load. Continuing southwards the journey was unhappily typical of con-temporary operating as over 10min were lost by signal and pw restrictions, despite this the arrival at Euston was only 1¼min late. The net overall time from Birmingham was 118min and the net start to stop time from Coventry to Euston was 94min for the 94 miles. The load was well in excess of that carried by the prewar two hour expresses. Over the traditional racing stretch from Welton to Willesden the net average speed was 67½mph, with 450 tons this did not quite attain to the standard of the redoubtable Patriot No 5959 which in 1933 averaged 70mph with 445 tons but it was a cheerful sign that prewar standards were being approached. An unrebuilt Patriot would never have been expected to emulate No 5959 in 1951.

Some of the finest running by Jubilee class engines on the LNWR main line was recorded by Norman Harvey. On one of these journeys Driver W. G. Pile and Fireman H. Wallis relieved Preston men at Crewe with the 11am Fridays only train from Windermere. The load was 430 tons and the Preston men said they had known better engines but by skilled driving and firing the 158·1 miles were run in 157min 30sec. This was an example of steady time gaining without any exceptional running. A heavier load of 475 tons full was timed

by Mr Harvey from Northampton to Euston. The train was the
4.5pm from Wolverhampton made up to 14 bogies hauled by No
45734 *Meteor*. There is a difficult start from Northampton to Roade
but skilful handling by Driver Thomas and Fireman Yates took the
heavy train past Hemel Hempstead 41·3 miles in 44min 50sec,
despite a pws at Kings Langley, Watford Junction was reached in
56min start to stop for the 48·4 miles. The 15 miles gently rising from
Bletchley to Tring took 13min 16sec, this compares with 13min
13sec by 5959 with 445 tons in 1933. Prewar standards could be said
to be regained by running of this quality. Driver Thomas used 24per
cent cut off, and the first regulator valve for most of the work. The
Jubilees were not usually driven with ultra short nominal cut offs
and, like many other locomotive types, they could produce the same
drawbar hps and equal economy by part throttle and late cut off.

In the summer of 1953 the first postwar two hour bookings were
restored between Euston and Birmingham. This was not quite the
equal of prewar running because before the war there had been
1hr 55min trains with the Coventry stop and one two hour train with
three stops. The trains in 1953 were generally heavier. The work of
the Bushbury engines on the postwar Birmingham Two Hour
expresses was one of the highspots of Jubilee performance and is
worthy of fuller treatment in a subsequent chapter.

Slowly over the country as a whole the prewar standards came
creeping back and in July 1948 the southbound "Postal" over the
Scottish Region had its booking restored to the prewar 68min for
the 57·3 heavily graded miles from Aberdeen to Forfar and to 34min
for the 32·5 miles from Forfar to Perth, a traditional racing ground
in the great days of the old Caledonian. These timings were improved
on by Jubilee class engines. In July 1948 Cecil J. Allen described some
running by No 5727 *Inflexible* and No 5732 *Sanspareil* that approxi-
mated to prewar standards. A better run was published in 1950 when
Cecil J. Allen published a run timed by R. H. Nelson with engine No
45580 *Burma* with a load of 315 tons. The 57·3 miles from Aberdeen
to Forfar were covered in 59¾min net and this was followed by a net
time of 29¾min net for the 32·5 miles from Forfar to Perth. The
maximum speed at the Tay Viaduct was 88½mph. In fairness it must
be recorded that work of an equally high standard was recorded by
Class Five engines.

It was however with the Midland section that the Jubilee class was
mainly associated. On the LNWR and the Caledonian they shared
the work with bigger engines that tended to overshadow them but
on the Midland south of Leeds they were the premier express type.

A most interesting example of the hard work performed by a Jubilee class engine on the Midland is given by O. S. Nock in *Four Thousand Miles on the Footplate* (Ian Allan 1952). Mr Nock rode on the footplate of No 45557 *New Brunswick* hauling 370 tons on the 10.15am from St Pancras to Manchester. The schedule was not difficult but with an 11 coach-load and restrained downhill speeds the uphill work was relatively hard south of Leicester and hard on the climb to Peak Forest. Coal consumption was heavy between Derby and Peak Forest and this raised the total figure for the journey. The engine steamed well throughout but the task of an engine crew facing the climb to Peak Forest with a shy steaming engine was not one to be envied. Engine crews should not be blamed for sometimes demanding a pilot after Derby.

The following table shows the process of restoring prewar standards on the Midland main line.

1945	No 5628	430 tons	Luton–Bedford	19·6 miles 21min 8sec Max 85
			Kettering–Oakham pass	21·8 miles 26min 32sec
1947	No 5663	230 tons	Leicester–St Pancras	99·1 miles 95min net
	No 5650	360 tons	Derby–Leicester	29·4 miles 30min 35sec
			Leicester–Luton	68·9 miles 75min net
			Luton–St Pancras	30·2 miles 32min 7sec
1951	No 45589	360 tons	St Pancras–Nottingham	123½ miles 130min net
1952	No 45657	360 tons	St Pancras–Leicester	99·1 miles 100min net
1953	No 45589	325 tons	Leicester–St Pancras	99·1 miles 95¾min net

The run by No 5663 *Jervis* was back to prewar standards as regards speed but the very light load of 230 tons reduced the merit of the run. The run by No 5650 *Blake* was of greater real merit and speeds such as a minimum of 51mph at Sharnbrook Summit and a maximum of 82mph at Radlett were higher than normal for 1947. The run to Nottingham in 1951 with engine No 45589 *Gwalior* featured a driver who had a very high reputation in the early 1950s Driver M. Robinson of Leeds. The minimum speeds at Sandridge and Sharnbrook were 55mph and 46mph respectively but perhaps the best running came near the end of the journey when a speed of 55mph was attained from the Melton slack up the 1 in 177 to Grimston after this the engine gave a taste of prewar standards by reaching 87½mph at Plumtree. The engine *Gwalior* was an excellent performer in the early 1950s and several notable runs were recorded and Driver Robinson had an equally distinguished record with engines of the Black Five class.

The load of 360 tons was typical of a Midland express in the early 1950s and with this load No 45657 *Tyrwhitt* ran from St Pancras to Leicester in 102min 22sec or 100min net while in 1953 Cecil J. Allen described a run with the redoubtable *Gwalior* which ran from Leicester to St Pancras in a net time of 95¾min. This was fully in the best prewar tradition but it would be over optimistic to claim that every Jubilee run was of the same quality. There were occasions when poor coal, run down engines and many delays caused bad time keeping. It will be noted that in order to indicate the improved engine working it had been necessary to quote net times in most cases. The public judged the railway by actual times and they still craved for private motoring.

Over the Leeds–Carlisle route the heaviest duties were taken by the Royal Scots but when a Jubilee was called upon for a special effort there were occasional runs of prewar standard. In March 1952 Cecil J. Allen described a run timed by a correspondent from the footplate of No 45619 *Nigeria* hauling 340 tons southwards from Carlisle. The run from Carlisle to Hellifield was performed in well under the scheduled allowance. The first stage, 30·8 miles to Appleby, was run in 36min 11sec. The engine was driven with a wide regulator opening and cut offs varying from 18 to 32per cent. Continuing beyond Appleby the train ran into a number of pwr slacks. To recover from the first of these up 1 in 100 the cut off was advanced to 38per cent with full regulator and from the second check 35per cent brought speed up to 43mph on the 1 in 100 to Smardale Viaduct. This was running approaching the quality of the *Rooke* trials but there was a slight easing on the upper section to Ais Gill which was passed at 33mph on 30per cent cut off. Boiler pressure was held well on the ascent. The water consumption was estimated at 3,700 gallons for the 76·8 miles; a similar total water consumption was estimated on a fast run with the same load over the 112·9 miles from Euston to Birmingham. This gives some indication of the greater difficulty of the northern banks.

On two Sundays in March 1955 trial runs were made with Jubilee and Black Five class engines over the Lickey Incline. The Class Five had seven bogies and the Jubilee had eight, each train included the dynamometer car. The Jubilee was No 45554 *Ontario* which had no difficulty in climbing the bank from a start at Stoke Works and 30mph through Bromsgrove station. On the second attempt a stop was made on the bank and *Ontario* failed to get away but after returning to the foot of the bank subsequent attempts were successful. The engine had no difficulty in climbing the bank with its 252-ton train from a stop in Bromsgrove station. These tests did not lead to any change in normal banking procedure.

Sometimes, at periods of heavy traffic, bankers were not always available when required and on a July Saturday afternoon in 1954 a party from the Leicester Railway Society on a photographic expedition assembled at the summit of the Lickey Incline. The whistle denoting the start from Bromsgrove yard was heard and time passed by as the roar of the northbound "Devonian" came wafting up the bank. Once there was a single burst of slipping which was quickly checked and the Jubilee came pounding on slowly but surely. Finally, 17min after the whistle, against a booking of 8min, No 45699 *Galatea* of Bristol shed breasted the summit followed by 14 corridor bogies weighing at least 480 tons and bringing up the rear, gallantly doing its best, was one "Jinty" No 47301. Each engine must have been handling as much as the test trains and the rails were damp. The expression of the fireman was not enthusiastic. With many miles still to run with a heavy load, his task with a fire torn to pieces was not an enviable one.

In 1957 the Midland introduced its XL timetable with a host of even time bookings. This timetable restored in large measure the prewar position. The operation of this timetable was not a complete success but in attempting to keep it the Jubilee class recorded some of its finest work. The running of the Birmingham trains and the Midland XL timetable represents the zenith of postwar performance by the class and as such deserves fuller treatment.

CHAPTER TEN

The zenith of postwar achievement

THE BIRMINGHAM 2hr expresses stood high in public esteem when the LNWR was at the height of its pride and it was perhaps appropriate that the Jubilees were used during the final years of steam haulage because the Webb Jubilees inaugurated the service. The Birmingham trains had seen the Precursors and the Georges at their best while some good work had been done by the compounds after a rather uncertain start. In an earlier chapter of this book we have seen how well the Patriots performed in the years leading up to World War II. In the early 1950s the Jubilees contributed their own page of the Birmingham story, a story that today is one of new brilliance as the AL6s run the 90min trains.

The Jubilees used on the Birmingham 2hr expresses came mainly from Bushbury shed with a few turns worked by Camden engines. Platform end gossips always claimed that the best of the class were stationed at Bushbury and it would certainly appear that these engines were the best maintained; the excellent condition of the Bushbury stud can be verified even today by reference to numerous published photographs. It was rumoured that Bushbury shed had a few redraughting tricks and this is not impossible because it has now been revealed that Kings Cross shed had discovered means of doctoring the single chimneyed A4s and what one railway could do is not impossible on another. Many of the star performers at Bushbury were of the final series with the 31sq ft grates but too much significance should not be attached to this single dimension because under working conditions the difference in effective operation of grates of 29·5 and 31sq ft can hardly be measured. Some of the finest runs recorded on the Midland were with the engines which retained the smaller grate but which had received the larger superheater and the modified blastpipes. The load limit for Class 6 engines on the LNWR XL limit timings was 350 tons, this meant 11 bogies unless 12 wheeled diners were used. The more usual formation was 10 bogies weighing 340-345 tons gross.

An interesting example of the work of a Jubilee on these trains was given by Cecil J. Allen in the *Railway Magazine* for September

THE BRISTOL-BIRMINGHAM MAIN LINE

No 45663 *Jervis* in a pastoral setting with an early morning Bristol-Bradford express near Westerleigh in June 1953. */G. F. Heiron*

Above: No 45679 *Armada* comes out of the autumn mists near Knighton Tunnel with the down "Palatine" in October 1957.
[J. F. Clay

Left: No 45606 *Falkland Islands* at Euston station as pilot to a Royal Scot on the up "Ulster Express" in August 1957. *[J. F. Clay*

Below: No. 45624 *St Helena* heads the up "Mancunian" express south of Rugby on the former LNWR main line.
[T. G. Hepburn

SOME NAMED
EXPRESSES

Class 2 4–4–0 No 40504 piloting Jubilee No 45667 *Jellicoe* across Harringworth viaduct with the down "Waverley". *[J. F. Clay*

Nos 45691 *Orion* and No 45573 *Newfoundland* passing Gargrave with the down "Waverley". *[Eric Treacy*

THE NORTH WALES LINE

No 45690 *Leander* leaving Chester General with a Liverpool-Llandudno excursion on Sunday August 12, 1962.

/D. Cross

THE ZENITH OF POSTWAR ACHIEVEMENT

1953. One of the runs was recorded by a correspondent on the footplate of the only unrebuilt double chimneyed Jubilee at that time No 45742 *Connaught*. The load was 340 tons and the double chimneyed engine made the run appear to be comparatively easy. For most of the journey the regulator handle was only half open, this was thought to correspond with a steam chest pressure of 165–185lb. Tring Summit was passed at 63mph on 20per cent cut off while 17per cent on the easy grades produced 78mph at Wolverton. There was a pwr check at Roade after which 28per cent cut off was used for the initial recovery, this was reduced to 15per cent after Blisworth and increased up the rise to Kilsby Tunnel to a final 22per cent where speed fell from 71 to 64mph. Coventry was reached in 92min 6sec or 88¼min net for the 94 miles. This very competent run was estimated as involving a water consumption of 3,700 gallons for the run to Birmingham and the coal was estimated at 42lb/mile.

The standard single chimneyed Jubilees had no difficulty in equalling the net time of the double chimneyed engine and in the same article Cecil J. Allen described two runs with similar net times by engine No 45733 *Novelty* which was a regular performer on the Two Hour expresses. It is possible to form a very reliable estimate of the capacity of a well handled Jubilee from a most extensive series of logs kindly lent by K. R. Phillips. The averages from a large number of logs are a better basis for comparison than single runs which may be influenced by special circumstances good or bad. It becomes possible to present the Jubilees in relation to the contemporary running standards of other LMR steam engines. In doing this care has to be taken not to read more into the results than the figures infer. There is, for example, no disposition to imply that the Jubilees were the equal of the Royal Scots which have to their credit feats of hill climbing well beyond Jubilee capacity. Performance is the product of design and operation and the comparative figures revealed by an analysis of K. R. Phillip's timings should be regarded as a tribute to the engine crews, mainly Bushbury men, concerned.

Euston–Rugby (82·6 miles)

Type of engine	No of runs	Average load	Average net time
Class 6 Jubilee ..	36	343 tons	81·02min
Class 7 Royal Scot ..	4	402 tons	83·87min
Class 8 Pacific ..	21	450 tons	80·26min

In the down direction it is possible to compare the work of the Jubilees on the Birmingham trains with the work of Class 7 and Class 8 engines on the 80min booking to Rugby of the down "Midday Scot".

E

The passing times of the down Birmingham trains have been corrected to the equivalent stopping time at Rugby.

The small number of runs by Class 7 engines reduces the comparative value as there are not enough runs to claim a representative sample. Class 7 engines were not normally employed on the down "Midday Scot". The 21 Pacific runs include trips by Duchesses, Princesses and the lone No 71000. The work of the Jubilees may justly be claimed to be roughly comparable, size for size, with that of the Pacifics but it must be emphasised that to achieve this result they would need to be worked closer to their maximum capacity. It would be most difficult for a fireman to stoke a Duchess at the same rate in lbs of coal per sq ft of grate area as was normal practice on a Jubilee. If the comparison was extended backwards it would doubtless be found that the Georges were worked harder, relatively, than the Jubilees. The larger the engine the easier it was for the designer to include features which made possible maximum power outputs and maximum efficiency but as long as the engines were hand fired the less likely it was to find it possible to sustain a maximum effort except in special test conditions.

The even time bookings to Coventry could be kept quite easily with the full 380 tons. K. R. Phillips timed No 45734 *Meteor* with the full 11 coach-load of 380 tons; the actual time was 93min 47sec and the net time 88½min. This was no unique effort as I was fortunate enough to time an almost precisely equal run by No 45733 *Novelty* in 93min 31sec or 89min net while further confirmation comes from similar runs in Norman Harvey's collection. With this load there was normally little gain in the 35min booking to passing Tring but an unchecked run could be 2min ahead of the 61min booking at Blisworth, 3min ahead at Rugby and 4min in front at the Coventry stop. This estimate is made from a number of runs and may be said fairly to represent a well handled Jubilee at its best in normal service conditions. Under special test conditions possibly a few more minutes could have been pared from the timings. A lighter load enabled a faster run to be made and Mr Phillips timed a run by No 45688 *Polyphemus* with a 9 coach-load of 310 tons gross. Coventry was reached in a net time of 84¾min while No 45741 *Leinster* took 87min net with 340 tons. The power output on these runs would be similar to that on the runs with the heavier loads.

The up direction was slightly easier than the down and both in prewar and postwar days more spectacular running was made with no greater power output. On the 94min booking up from Coventry K. R. Phillips logged enough runs for averages to be made but again there were hardly enough Class 7 runs to make the comparison significant.

Coventry-Euston (94 miles)

Type of engine	No of runs	Average load	Average net time
Class 6 Jubilee ..	16	356 tons	89·1min
Class 7 Royal Scot	4	366 tons	90·06min

A more interesting comparison is possible on the 79min booking from Rugby to Euston of the 2.30pm up from Birmingham which was, for a time, the fastest booking on LMR metals.

Rugby-Euston (82.6 miles)

Type of engine	No of runs	Average load	Average net time
Class 6 Jubilee ..	14	360 tons	76·9min
Class 7 Royal Scot or Reblt Patriot	14	366 tons	75·6min

The Jubilees doubtless had to be worked harder than the Class 7s to achieve this result. This train was sometimes worked by a Camden Jubilee with Bushbury men. Two of the best runs recorded by K. R. Phillips were with No 45737 *Atlas* which made net times of 74¾min with 355 tons and 76min net with 370 tons. A rather faster run was published by O. S. Nock in the November 1964 *Railway Magazine* when the engine No 45738 *Samson* achieved a net time of 72¾min with 365 tons. One of the highest power outputs was that when No 45737 *Atlas* had to deal with a 430-ton train without a pilot, the engine covered the 82·6 miles in an actual time of 77min 43sec or 76½min net. Driver Wooten of Bushbury shed and his fireman deserve every credit for such a run. It was published by Cecil J. Allen in the March 1957 *Railway Magazine*. Perhaps the fastest time on record with steam for a postwar Birmingham express was made when Black Five No 45287 was turned out as pilot to Jubilee No 45555 *Quebec* with a 12-coach train of 410 tons gross. The fun was fast and furious and the net time was 70min start to stop while the famous Welton to Willesden racing ground of prewar days was covered at an average speed of 79·4mph for the 69·9 miles. The modest summits at Roade and Tring were passed at 73 and 70mph while the maximum downhill was 88mph at Kings Langley. This was not quite as fast as the run by the Jubilee and the Patriot described in Chapter 5 but it was not far behind and the pace was distinctly hot for the mixed traffic engine which led the way.

There are enough good runs detailed in this chapter to establish the Jubilees as engines of some merit and nothing should be allowed to dim the glory of these runs nor should anything detract from the credit due to the engine crews. At the same time it must be recorded that not all Jubilee running on the LNWR was at the same level. The work of the Jubilees on the Birmingham services was however, with little doubt, the most consistent high speed running recorded by the class in the postwar world. The possible reasons for this were, the selection of some of the best engines in the class for Bushbury shed, the excellent condition in which many of them were maintained, the talented crews that drove and fired the engines and perhaps the easy grades of the old LNWR route called for an even, rather than a fluctuating steaming rate, which proved to be to the liking of the engines.

The most spectacular running involving the highest maximum speeds but also, alas, some of the most erratic running took place on the Midland main line. The introduction of the XL timetable in the summer of 1957 was a venturesome move which was not altogether a success. There had been a number of 60mph bookings for a year or two before but there proved to be a world of difference between managing a few fast bookings each day and making the former optimum standard of running the everyday normal standard over the whole train service. The Jubilees were older than they were in 1937, the coal was of a more variable quality and at times could be very bad and the loads were, on the average, heavier than they had been in prewar days. The load limit for a Jubilee on the fastest bookings was the same 300 tons but in prewar days many of the fast trains were only loading to 7 or 8 bogies while in 1957 it was rare for loads to fall below 9 coaches which, if modern BR stock was included, meant some slight excess over the official limit. The general standard of timekeeping was poor as those of us who did any lineside photography will remember and there was frequent and adverse comment in the local evening papers. The railway image in the Midlands was deteriorating and modernisation was only in its very early stages. Locomotive inspectors were sent ranging far and wide on Jubilee footplates and the desks of Authority groaned under the weight of their reports. Locomotive enthusiasts would like to think that all bad timekeeping was the result of bad operating and unnecessary signal and pw delays; there were plenty of these on the Midland but the cause of late running which headed the list was bad steaming.

There must have been many others who shared my own disappointment when an engine outwardly clean and capable looking staggered uphill at 40mph or lower and drifted downhill at a miserable 65 which did nothing to aid recovery. On other occasions however, a dirty old warrior of a Jubilee with an unpromising 3,500 gallon tender might turn up a performance of surprising merit. The uncertainty of performance that, in retrospect at least, seems to have added such interest to train timing was a great worry to the responsible authorities. They were at first reluctant to believe the evidence of their inspectors but as the weight of evidence accumulated some action was essential. Serious attempts were made to improve the standard of coal available for the XL bookings but this had little effect. In October 1957 some Royal Scots were drafted to the Midland for the Manchester services followed by some Britannias. These larger engines should have given much needed relief and some of the best runs of the Class 7 engines were better than anything recorded by the Jubilees but the average standard fell short of expectations. Perhaps the same story of the poorer engines of the class being posted to another region was reinacted, this had happened before when the poorer Claughtons were sent to the Midland in the 1920s and the worn out A3s were sent to the GCR in the 1940s. There was a lot of double heading with the ancient Midland Class 2 4-4-0s officiating as pilots. These old veterans should have been allowed to have lived out the evening of their lives on gentle tasks near to the homestead but they were called out and made to ride with the posse. Not only did they have to travel far but they had to travel faster than they ever should have done at their age. There are hair-raising tales told of fire irons going over the side, of motion dropped at high speed and of happenings which recall the wild tales of the old G&SWR told in his inimitable manner by D. L. Smith. For a short time the Standard Class 4 4-6-0s were used as pilots and although they could perhaps run as fast as the old 4-4-0s the pace was too hot for their 5ft 8in wheels to accept with comfort.

There were suggestions that SR Schools class 4-4-0s were to be sent to the LMR to act as pilots on the Midland section trains and that West Country class Pacifics were to try their hand on the XL bookings. There is little doubt that a West Country with its excellent boiler and good riding reputation would have proved to be at least the equal of the Royal Scots and Britannias in sustained and maximum speeds south of Leicester. On the climb to Peak Forest their boiler power might have resulted in some very fast climbs in dry weather but in a bleak Derbyshire winter a class of Pacific which was light on its feet might have been rather different. Authority was perhaps wise in not accepting the suggestion however much it may be regretted by the enthusiast who waited with camera and stop watch. Finally it was decided to seek a final solution of the problem of poor steaming by accelerating the diesel programme. The mass introduction of relatively untried diesels caused considerable trouble at first but today the Midland main line enjoys a service which puts the 1957 XL timetable in the shade.

Having accepted the fact that the standard of Jubilee running was very variable during the final years of steam operation it is also fair to record the fact that the Jubilees were not complete failures on the fast bookings. The best runs recorded were very good and there were sufficient of them to form a representative sample. The greatest credit must be given to the engine crews who drove and fired the engines with such resolution as to leave an impressive record of maximum achievement.

One of the routes on which a large number of performances are fully documented by reliable train timers is the down road from St Pancras to Kettering where the schedule was 71min for the 72 miles. The average net time of 23 runs recorded by K. R. Phillips works out at 69·07min for the 72 miles with an average load of 325 tons. From this analysis and from a large number of confirmatory runs in Norman Harvey's collection, it can be established that a well handled Jubilee in good condition could be expected to cover 62–63 miles in the first hour from St Pancras with the maximum XL load of 325 gross tons. It would be possible under optimum test conditions to raise this to 66–67 miles. This compares with the present day standard of running with "Peak" Class 46 diesels and the same 9 coach-load; today it is normal to cover 76–78 miles in the first hour from St Pancras. Doubtless a "Peak" with unrestricted downhill speeds would cover over 80 miles in the first hour but neverthless the average Jubilee figure is a creditable one for a design which dates back to 1934 and which was intended to have no more than two-thirds of the horse-power of today's diesels.

On a good run by a Jubilee hauling 9 bogies on the down road a minimum speed of 50–55mph would be expected at Elstree up 1 in 176, speed would then rise to around 75mph at Radlett and fall to 60mph at Sandridge Box after 4 miles of 1 in 176, speed would then remain in the lower 70s over the undulating stretch to Leagrave after which it would rise to between 85 and 90mph on the 1 in 200 descent to Bedford. The impetus of the high speed would carry the train over the 1 in 119 to MP 59¾ at slightly over 50mph. After this an even time finish at Kettering was easily possible with speed rising to 75 before the Wellingborough slack and reaching 67–68mph before shutting off steam for Kettering. On some of the best runs speeds of 62–64 were recorded at Sandridge and up to 58mph at

MP 59¾, the speed here depending as much on the initial impetus as on the horse-power developed on the bank.

The maximum speed reached on the descent from Luton to Bedford was always the most exciting feature of a down run on the Midland but it was not always the most significant piece of locomotive performance. It would appear that if a Jubilee was driven normally downhill speed would exceed 85mph on the two stretches of 1 in 200 but if extended a little more speed would rise to over 90mph. Personally I was never lucky enough to time anything higher than 88mph but K. R. Phillips has recorded 97½mph near MP 48 with engine No 45579 *Punjab* and a load of 320 tons. I have heard of another 97mph maximum by a reliable recorder and Mr Phillips has recorded 96mph by 45597 *Barbados* with 325 tons while in the February 1958 *Railway Magazine* Cecil J. Allen described a run with a maximum speed of 96mph attained by No 45654 *Hood* also with 325 tons. This run was timed by H. J. J. Griffith. Speeds of 93–94mph have frequently been recorded. It would appear that somewhere between 95 and 100 a Jubilee reached a critical maximum. A locomotive inspector with considerable experience of the engines tells me they needed pushing to go up into the 90s.

Having got as near as 97½ to the magic 100, we cannot completely rule out the possibility that it might have happened when all the operating conditions were favourable. There have been plenty of rumours of 100mph speeds with Jubilees and plenty of footplate men who claim to have seen 100mph on the speedometer but speedometers frequently read on the high side as a matter of policy and it must be recorded with regret that an authentic Jubilee 100 has not come to light. The speeds in the 95–97 mph range are fully supported by station to station timings.

The up road from Kettering to St Pancras also had bookings of 71min and here two of the best runs took place before the introduction of the 1957 XL timetable. The 2.26pm from Kettering to St Pancras was given the 73min booking and Mr Phillips timed two runs one in 1955 and one in 1956 with 11 coach-loads of 375 and 390 tons respectively. The engines were Nos 45627 and 45694 and the net times were 68 and 68¼min. These were excellent performances with these loads. An excellent run with a heavy load in unfavourable weather condition was recorded by Mr Phillips on the down 10.15am St Pancras to Glasgow with a load of 10 bogies, 375 tons, behind No 45658 *Keyes*. The train reached Leicester 8min late after two stops one for 33sec and the other for 3min 9sec at MP 27½ and two pwr slacks. The minimum speed at Elstree was 51mph and the creditable figure of 59mph was recorded at Sandridge. Other uphill speeds were 48½ at MP 59¾, 47 at Desborough and 53 at Kibworth while 87mph was reached downhill. The net time to Leicester was 96½min, a remarkable performance with a 375-ton load equal in power output to anything recorded before the war. The speeds through Market Harborough and round the Wigston North Junction curve were however somewhat higher than the stipulated limits. In general the speeds round the various curves were more strictly kept in prewar days than in the days of the 1957 XL timetable.

There is an especially interesting basis for comparison in the running recorded on the up road from Leicester to St Pancras because a number of engine classes have been recorded over this route under similar conditions and it is possible to place the Jubilee class in the position it has gained for itself. It is also possible to compare the best Jubilee postwar work with the best recorded before the war detailed in Chapter 7. Care has to be taken, however, to allow for the more stringent observation of service slacks which was the normal practice before the war. The net times in the following table have been adjusted to put pre and postwar runs on a common basis, this accounts for them being in some cases slightly different from figures published elsewhere.

Leicester–St Pancras (99·1 miles)

Prewar	Black Five	4–6–0	260 tons	91min net
	Jubilee	4–6–0	235 tons	84min net
	Jubilee	4–6–0	302 tons	89min net
Postwar	Black Five	4–6–0	280 tons	90min net
	Jubilee	4–6–0	265 tons	85min net
	Jubilee	4–6–0	330 tons	89min net
	73000	4–6–0	330 tons	92min net
	Reb Patriot	4–6–0	330 tons	86min net
	Britannia	4–6–2	355 tons	88min net
	Class 46 "Peak" diesel		290 tons	76min net

The above net times have been corrected to the nearest minute and it is possible for experienced time recorders to question their detail but it is submitted that the comparative values are sound. The fastest postwar run was timed by K. R. Phillips and the engine No 45636 *Uganda* ran up from Leicester in a net time given above as 85min. This was a performance equal in merit to the prewar run of No 5622 which is the fastest net time on record with steam. The times from Bedford North Junction up to Luton were 15min 21sec for 5622 and 16min 1sec for 45636, the postwar engine had 30tons more so, given neutral atmospheric conditions in both cases, the merit was not significantly different. It may fairly be concluded from the above table that:

1. The Jubilees at their best could equal the best prewar standards in the more difficult postwar world.
2. The Jubilees at their best could compare reasonably well, size for size, with the best runs of other steam engines used on the Midland main line.

As a point of general interest it may be added that the Jubilee responsible for the excellent run in 89min net with 330 tons was No 45589 *Gwalior* the hero of some excellent runs in the previous chapter.

The same general pattern was followed on other routes where Jubilee class engines were used. In the *Railway Magazine* for September 1959 O. S. Nock published a table of runs on the 21min booking for the 20·8 miles from Leicester to Trent. The fastest run with engine No 45682 *Trafalgar* and 310 tons took 20min 7sec start to stop with a maximum speed of 83mph at Loughborough; the slowest took 20min 56sec with a maximum of 77mph. This again showed that a Jubilee was a reasonably competent engine on a sharp start to stop run over easy grades.

Some indication of the best postwar work of Jubilees over the fierce grades up to Peak Forest was given in the article published by Cecil J. Allen in the March 1960 *Trains Illustrated*. The Jubilee class engine No 45616 *Malta GC*, driven by Driver H. Edwards and fired by Fireman B. Thomas of Kentish Town shed, a crew that had many fine achievements to their credit, was hauling a load of 290 tons. Speed did not fall below 47mph on the 1 in 100 from Rowsley and it was excellent work to attain 45mph up 1 in 90 from the Millers Dale start. The fact that the Britannia class engine No 70014, with the same crew, attained 53mph at Peak Forest does not detract from the merit of the Jubilee performance, as size for size, the two climbs are of equal merit. The run of *Malta GC* through the Peak district showed that twenty years after the famous test runs of *Rooke* the same standards of uphill work could be attained.

It is of course true, as has been shown earlier, that the Jubilees did not always give of their established best in normal service conditions in the late 1950s but this was also true of a number of famous locomotive classes on the LMR and other regions. It may have been that the amplitude of variation was particularly high with the Jubilees but they were worked on rather tight margins. The standard of work needed for the bare timekeeping of the Midland

XL bookings was closer to the test maximum output of a Jubilee than anything the timetable asked of a Duchess in comparison with the performance on test of No 6234 in 1939. We can at least honour the engine crews who made possible the maximum efforts recorded on the Birmingham Two Hour Expresses and the best runs on the Midland in the final years of steam. Nevertheless the introduction of more Class 7 engines on the hardest bookings was fully justified and with diesel traction forecast in the 1955 Modernisation Programme the decline of the Jubilee class in the 1960s was inevitable.

CHAPTER ELEVEN

The declining years

THE RAILWAY MODERNISATION PLAN of 1955 foreshadowed the end of steam on British railways but at first the intention was to run steam down gradually while diesel prototypes were tested and sound designs for future standardisation were selected. Many people still think this would have been a wiser policy but the continuing worsening of the commercial viability of the industry led to an acceleration of the pace of dieselisation almost to the point of panic. At one time it looked as if anything on wheels that was diesel driven could be sure of a place on the railway. It is possible that erratic steaming by a number of steam types in use in large numbers may also have contributed to the decision to end steaming troubles by ending steam.

Such was the climate of railway policy when Jubilee class engine No 45722 was sent to the Rugby Test Plant late in 1956 to see what could be done to improve the reliability of the class. The results are given by E. S. Cox in *Chronicles of Steam* (Ian Allan 1967) and the figures, as they stand, do not flatter the class. It was found that in steady steaming on the Plant the front end limit of 45722 was reached at an evaporation rate of 20,760lb/hr. This was actually less than the corresponding figure for the later Stanier Black Five class engines which had a smaller boiler but a better general reputation for steaming. At the maximum rate of evaporation No 45722 needed firing at the rate of 3,324lb/hr and the sustained ihp was 1,350.

It may be asked how this figure of 1,350 can be reconciled with the maximum ihps of 1,800 or over given in connection with the 1937 trials of No 5660 *Rooke?* The answer is that:

1. The figures given in 1937 were maximum ihp figures sustained perhaps for one minute only while the figure of 1,350 in the 1956/7 trials was steadily maintained. The Duchess class engine No 6234 reached 3,300ihp as a transitory maximum while 2,700 was the sustained maximum on the Plant.
2. Engines could frequently reach a somewhat higher maximum rate of evaporation on the road than on the Plant because vibration

assisted evaporation. The test results of the Britannia bear this out. 3. In 1937 No 5660 was a newer engine and may have had better coal.

The evaporation figure given for No 5660 during the two days trial running in December 1937 was 18,750lb/hr between Bristol and Leeds and 19,500 between Leeds and Bristol. These figures are evidence of the fact that 5660 was worked at a rate close to its test house maximum. On the northbound run in 1937 the water evapor-rated/lb/coal was 6·26lb closely in conformity with the 6·25/lb/coal measured on the Plant. On the southbound run the water/lb/coal of 5660 was 6·86lb/coal, this was a rather better figure but it was not a good result and it suggested that 5660 was pressed harder than was desirable in ordinary service.

The results of the Rugby tests and a critical re-examination of the prewar test figures suggested that the boiler proportions and the draughting could be modified with advantage.

The test engineers experimented by redesigning the blastpipe and chimney assembly on the lines suggested by the results of redraughting modifications by S. O. Ell at Swindon. The blastpipe diameter was increased from $4\frac{3}{4}$in to $5\frac{1}{2}$in but the blastpipe top was placed nearer to the chimney base and the inside taper of the chimney choke was altered from 1 in 7 to 1 in 14. These were small changes but they raised the maximum evaporation rate to 25,000lb/hr. A steaming rate of 25,000lb/hr was, of course, good for a boiler of these dimensions but the result had been obtained at a high cost because the firing rate had been increased to 4,435lb/hr. Such a rate could hardly be expected in regular service for many minutes from a single fireman. Tests on the Swindon Plant and on the road in 1949 with a Castle fitted with the 3-row superheater showed an apparently higher boiler efficiency with an evaporation rate of 24,000lb/hr on a firing rate of 3,200lb/hr. The calorific value of the coal used would be higher in the Castle tests and the degree of superheat was greater in the Jubilee test. This would suggest that if the Castle and the Jubilee were tested on a basis of coal per dbhp the difference would be less than is the case in a comparison based on boiler evaporation alone. The highest ihp recorded by the Castle was 1,810ihp at a steam consumption rate of 28,000lb/hr, above the steady evaporation rate. It is doubtful if the 1,800ihps of No 5660 *Rooke* were ever exceeded by a single chimney Castle though a double chimney 4-row superheater Castle could possibly have done so. The fact remained however that the Jubilee test results indicated the need for a redesigning of the boiler tubes to give better efficiency and more superheat. The double chimney on the Jubilee made possible the 25,000lb/hr evaporation rate on a much lower blastpipe pressure but the degree of superheat was disappointing. This again suggested that there was need for a modified tube layout. The point had been reached where further advantages from front end modifications could not be expected to yield results. Better steaming could have been obtained by more drastic boiler alterations but at this late stage in steam locomotive history, when the diesel was just appearing over the horizon, it was decided that there was no great advantage to be gained from further capital expenditure on a form of motive power with a short life expectancy.

Nine engines were given the modified front end while keeping the single chimney. They could perform more work but at the expense of higher coal consumption. A locomotive inspector, with wide experience of the class, said that the main advantage of the modified engines was that the fire burnt more evenly over the whole grate. The maximum evaporation rate of 25,000lb/hr was rather an academic figure because no fireman could ever have kept it up for long. If they could have done so the Midland XL timetable could have been kept with loads of over 400 tons. A case could have been made out however for fitting more of the engines with the modified front end because it might have made possible higher short term power outputs when recovering time uphill and it might have reduced the amount of time lost by bad steaming on jobs requiring a normal power output. As things were the Jubilees had to soldier on as they were in a world where no one was interested in their welfare.

Even before the Jubilees were replaced by diesels on their top link duties the best had passed. Double heading on the Midland increased, sometimes the older ex-Midland engines of the Class 2 or compound classes officiated but age was beginning to tell and sometimes the assistance was of limited value. There were however the occasional runs that were a great credit to the veteran pilots. This was the case when Class 2 No 40682 assisted Jubilee No 45561 with a 400-ton train, a net time of 91min was made from Leicester to St Pancras with a maximum speed of 85 at East Langton and 86½ at Sharnbrook. The fastest double headed runs however took place when Black Fives or 73s acted as pilots. Before the diesel take over more Class 7 engines of the Royal Scot or Britannia classes were used on the Midland. The general improvement was perhaps disappointing but there were significant indications of what might have happened if Class 7s had been used earlier. A Royal Scot reached

Kettering in a net time of 71min with 450 tons and another topped Sandridge at 72mph nearly 10mph more than the Jubilee "best" with the same 320-ton load. On the Leeds–Carlisle route the LMS types were supplanted briefly by Gresley A3 class Pacifics before the diesels finally took over. The A3 class engine No 60082 *Neil Gow* with a 300-ton train showed its ability to sustain just over 50mph on the 1 in 100 up to Blea Moor against the 45 by *Rooke* in 1937. The Jubilee had, however, not been outclassed on a size for size basis by the larger A3. A hill climbing performance that was relatively, as well as actually, better than that of *Rooke* had to wait until some special efforts were made on enthusiasts' rail tours with a Duchess in 1961 and with A4s in 1967.

With diesels beginning to show themselves and with Class 7 steam engines on the faster and heavier turns, the Jubilees on the Midland found their duties a little easier but before they went there were a few moments of glory. In August 1959 test runs were made to examine the feasibility of proposed timings for the diesel Midland Pullman that it was hoped to introduce. The Jubilee class engine No 45585 *Hyderabad* hauling two corridor bogies and a track testing coach passed Kettering in 60min for the 72 miles, Leicester in 84min after which a pw check made the time to passing Derby over two hours but Manchester was reached on time in 3¼hrs from St Pancras. The return journey was made next day in 3hr 10min. Some of the point to point timings on these tests must have been the fastest ever performed by steam on the Midland but the light load would detract from its value as a locomotive performance.

On all railways there were occasions when locomotives found themselves faced with tasks far more difficult than anything normally expected. Such was the case when Jubilee No 45561 *Saskatchewan* had to work the up "Palatine" with a load of 400 tons without the pilot to which the driver was entitled. The 29·3 miles from Derby to Leicester were run in 30min 16sec but this good running was excelled by running from Leicester to St Pancras 99·1 miles in an actual time of 98min 49sec or 91min net. As sometimes happened when an exceptional effort was made in postwar days there was a somewhat liberal interpretation of the Market Harborough slack but this resulted in the excellent minimum of 52½mph at Desborough Box; the minimum of 56mph at MP 59¾, after 71, at Irchester was remarkable for a Jubilee with 400 tons. The ascent from Bedford to Luton might have been most revealing from the sustained hp angle but a signal check to 12mph at Millbrook spoilt the climb. It was good work to recover to 50mph on the 1 in 200 up to MP 34. Downhill speeds were 82½ at East Langton, 85 at Glendon, 86½ at Sharn-brook and 86½ before Hendon. This run was published by Cecil J. Allen in *Trains Illustrated* for October 1960 and was timed by M. G. Langdon. It may have taken place rather earlier in which case it should more correctly, have appeared in the previous chapter but it seems a particularly appropriate swan song for the Jubilee class on the Midland main line. The maximum hps must have approached those of the immortal *Rooke* in 1937.

As the diesels took over, the Jubilees dropped to semi-fasts and parcels trains and these were in demand from young photographers anxious to get pictures before it was too late. In June 1964 an immaculate Jubilee was once more seen on the Midland main line when No 45721 *Impregnable* headed a LCGB rail tour. The photographers were out in force and 45721 is reputed to have run very well with speeds up to 90mph. Jubilees were called out for holiday extras all over the system and photographers, who a few years earlier would put away their cameras in disgust with the words "Only another Jubilee", were, in the mid-1960s, making marathon journeys to photograph the surviving members of the class. This culminated with the two survivors at Holbeck making weekly journeys over Ais Gill greatly sought after by the photographers.

The same story can be told of the Jubilees on the former LNWR section. The bulk of the Birmingham traffic was transferred to the WR because of electrification work on the line to Euston and this ended the work of the Bushbury men on the Two Hour Expresses which was the most consistent running of the class in postwar days. In the January 1963 *Railway Magazine* O. S. Nock described some running on the Preston to Carlisle route on the Liverpool and Manchester to Glasgow trains. Jubilees shared in this work but they did not always seem able to stand the 70min hard steaming from Preston to Shap. Jubilees sometimes ran better at different parts of the same journey, at times a good ascent of Grayrigg Bank would be followed by a call for the banker at Tebay but on a journey by No 45665 *Lord Rutherford of Nelson* with 390 tons a moderate ascent of Grayrigg Bank was followed by the engine getting a "second wind" and climbing to Shap at a minimum of 27mph. In the southbound direction No 45593 *Kolhapur* with 335 tons sustained 39½mph on the long 1 in 125 while No 45718 *Dreadnought* with 320 tons sustained 41½mph at the same spot. These runs represented about 85per cent of the *Rooke* optimum standard.

The use of Jubilees south of Crewe dwindled to secondary trains as the diesels entered service but before the story is ended some brief mention should be made of the use of the Rebuilt Jubilee with the larger boiler No 45736 *Phoenix* on the most glamorous of LMR expresses the "Caledonian". The up afternoon "Caledonian" was handed over to No 45736 after the failure of a Pacific and the 4-6-0 had to work through to Euston with a stop at Stafford. The 165·5 miles from Carlisle to Stafford were covered in 161min but from Stafford to Euston the run was timed in detail, the 133·6 miles took 113min 34sec or 111½min net.

Jubilees had made sporadic appearances on the GC main line on Cup Final specials and such like jobs but during their final years they became much more regular performers. They were used at times on the Car Sleepers from Masborough to Marylebone via the Midland Beighton Junction and over the LD&ECR but they were never happy nor very popular on the GC especially on the grades north of Nottingham. In the mid-1960s they were frequent visitors to Nottingham or Leicester on holiday trains heading for Bournemouth. They were much sought after by photographers on these jobs.

As their use in normal service declined the Jubilees were in demand for enthusiasts' specials. From the large number of these workings that took place it is perhaps appropriate to select one rail tour as a suitable farewell to this part of the Jubilee story. On Sunday October 2, 1966 the SLS ran "The Pennine Rail Tour" from Birmingham (Snow Hill) via Crewe and Leeds to Carlisle. The engine used on the Leeds-Carlisle road was Jubilee No 45593 *Kolhapur* which is now preserved at Tyseley. The load was the XL limit of 300 tons and the 113 miles from Leeds to Carlisle were run in an actual time of 132min 20sec or 122½min net. Speed fell to 36mph on the 1 in 100 of the "Long Drag" but recovered on the slight easing of the grade near Ribblehead to enter Blea Moor Tunnel at 41mph. The maximum on the descent was 82mph. On the return journey Carlisle to Hellifield 76·6 miles took 90min 59sec or 88min net, Ais Gill was passed in 62min 53sec from Carlisle. The minimum speed on the 1 in 100 was 36mph. This performance was not quite the equal of *Rooke* but it was a creditable effort for an ageing engine.

A chequered history has now ended and we may ask what will be the verdict of future historians. They will not be able to claim, with any conviction, that the Jubilees were the best express engines ever to have run in this country but they may number them among the most interesting. They certainly had their faults the worst being erratic steaming, the cure for which was only discovered at a time too late for a remedy. Footplate crews were always worried by

No 45698 *Mars*, with small tender
leaving Sowerby Bridge with a
Liverpool-Newcastle train.   *[Eric Treacy*

No 45698 *Mars* at Manchester
Victoria with a train from York.
[J. R. Carter

THE LANCASHIRE
AND YORKSHIRE
MAIN LINE

No 45742 *Connaught* on up
Birmingham 2hr express near
Watford   [*British Railways*

No 45596 *Bahamas* on down fitted
freight near Shap Summit.
                [*T. G. Hepburn*

DOUBLE CHIMNEYS

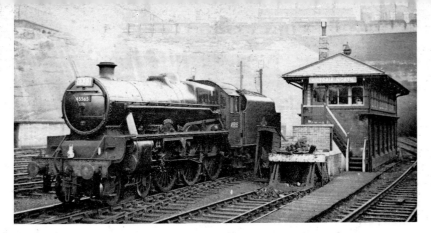

No 45565 *Victoria* at Nottingham
Victoria after working a special on
August 8, 1965.   *[H. A. Gamble*

THE FINAL YEARS

Above: The rebuilt Jubilee No 45735
Comet, unofficially renamed "Mick",
on up semi-fast from Nottingham
to Marylebone at Leicester GC,
April 1964.   *[T. G. Hepburn*

Below: No 45735 heading south out
of Leicester Central with an up
semi-fast for Marylebone.   *[C. P. Walker*

ONE OF THEIR LAST MAIN DUTIES

No 45593 *Kolhapur* near Dent with the 10.17am Leeds–Glasgow on July 29, 1967. An 8F with a southbound freight can be seen in the background about to cross Arten Gill Viaduct. *[Paul Riley*

unreliable injectors and here it is to be regretted that the Swindon pattern was not used from the start. The steaming troubles were aggravated by the cyclic workings which asked a lot of any hand fired design of moderate size. They looked better on paper to the accountant at his desk than to the fireman with his shovel.

In spite of everything, however, the Jubilee class had its moments of glory, the greatest being the climb over Ais Gill by *Rooke* which is sure of lasting fame as one of the classics of steam locomotive performance. The engines rode well and gave less trouble from cracked frames than some more powerful 4-6-0s. They were strong enough, on occasions, to stand up to merciless hammering. A comparison with the GWR Castles, with marks given for speed, consistency and economy, would doubtless result in a win on points for Swindon but if sheer horse-power is taken as the sole criterion, then *Rooke's* 1,800ihp was never excelled by a Castle by any significant amount. In this respect the earlier story of the Claughton and the Star was reinacted. We may ask what would have been the reputation of the Jubilees today if the LMS had run a super express limited to 250 tons from Euston to Birmingham in 105min hauled by selected Jubilees of low mileage. A record similar to that of the "Bristolian" might well have been achieved.

Conjecture, however, knows no limits and it has been shown in terms of recorded fact that, at their best, the Jubilees did much that was worthy of praise. Our admiration goes out to the men, especially the firemen, who made these things possible.

F

CHAPTER TWELVE

A Jubilee miscellany

BUILDING

THE JUBILEE CLASS eventually totalled 191 locomotives, 113 of which were built straight off the drawing board during 1934. E. S. Cox in *Locomotive Panorama Vol 1* tells of the intense efforts at Derby to complete a batch of 10 of these engines before the end of 1934. It is believed that the building of the intended 113 was complete before the end of 1934 though a few did not actually enter traffic before 1935. The urgency of Stanier's policy of restocking and standardisation may be judged by the fact that four separate erecting shops were engaged in construction simultaneously, namely the LMS works of Crewe and Derby together with the Queen's Park and Hyde Park works of the North British Locomotive Company in Glasgow. In would appear that No 5552 was completed at Crewe in April 1934 and entered traffic early in May.

The remaining 78 locomotives entered traffic during the period December 1935 to December 1936; all of these were outshopped from Crewe in sequence. There was a gap of some ten months between the initial batches, 5552–5664, and the final 78 locomotives during which time the boilers had been redesigned. The earlier engines at first had domeless boilers carrying top feed while the second series had top feed forward of the dome. Earlier engines were later converted to the domed pattern. The construction programme may be summarised:

Built 1934—5552-6 (Crewe) 5557-81 (Hyde Park, Glasgow); 5582-5606 (Queen's Park, Glasgow); 5607-5654 (Crewe) and 5655-64 (Derby).
Built 1935—5665-81 (Crewe)
Built 1936—5682-5742 (Crewe)

In all 131 were built at Crewe, 10 at Derby, 25 at Hyde Park and 25 at Queen's Park.

Although the whole class was built in a space of two and a half years it presented a completely non-standard appearance embracing four types of tender, two boiler outlines, three styles of livery, a change from the original nameless state and some individual engines with experimental modifications.

82

WITHDRAWAL

With the exception of 45637, damaged beyond repair in the Harrow disaster of October 1952 (officially withdrawn in December 1952), the first example to be withdrawn from normal service was 45609 in September 1960 after a life of 25½ years. The last to go was 45562 in November 1967 after 33 years service. Withdrawal was recorded as under:

1952—1; 1960—1; 1961—3; 1962—41; 1963—31; 1964—66; 1965— 33; 1966—7; 1967—8.

The largest monthly total was in December 1962 when 28 were withdrawn in one fell swoop which included 11 from Scotland thus rendering the class extinct north of the border.

The class became extinct from the regions on the following dates: LMR Western Div (Aug 1966); LMR Midland Div (Nov 1964); LMR Central Div (Jan 1967); Eastern Region (Dec 1962); NE Region (ER from 1/1/67) (Nov 1967); Scottish Region (Dec 1962), and Western Region (June 1964).

At the time of writing (December 1969) four of the class still remain, 5593 and 5596 preserved and restored to LMS livery for occasional steaming and 45690 and 45699 languishing in a South Wales scrapyard, both withdrawn in 1964.

BOILERS

As will be apparent from earlier chapters the original boilers fitted to the Jubilee class were not efficient steamers. Various experimental modifications were soon introduced in attempts to improve the steaming. The original domeless boilers had two rows of 7 superheater elements but the earlier examples of the second batch, built December 1935 onwards, had 3 rows of 7 elements and the final examples had 3 rows of 8 elements. The later engines had fireboxes with a grate area of 31sq ft against the original 29·5sq ft. One experimental boiler with 4 rows of 7, 28 elements, was built. This boiler was noted as being carried by engine No 45686 from September 1950—January 1954 and was later on 45685.

	Original 5552–5664	Intermediate 5665–5701	Final 5702–5742
Boiler dimensions			
Heating surface			
	sq ft	sq ft	sq ft
Firebox ..	162·4	181·1	181·1
Tubes ..	1462·5	1391	1466
Superheater	227	235	307
No of elements	14	21	24
Grate area	29·5	31	31

The original engines, built with domeless boilers, were later fitted with domed boilers with 24 element superheaters while retaining their 29·5sq ft grates. Many of the best recorded performances, including the test runs of No 5660 *Rooke*, were made by engines of this type. Five boilers with 21 elements remained domeless and were noted as being still in use in the 1950s.

Blastpipe diameter was originally 5⅛in with jumper blastpipe top. The jumper tops were fixed down on many engines and reductions were made for experimental purposes to 5in, 4⅞in, 4¾in and 4½in. Officially the standard diameter was fixed at 4¾in. This was increased to 5½in with modifications to the chimney choke after tests on engine No 45722 at Rugby Test Plant in 1956/7. Nine engines were given this modification. These were 45601, 45606, 45610, 45622, 45628, 45672, 45688, 45733 and 45738.

A Kylchap blastpipe and double chimney was fitted to No 5684 *Jutland* in 1937. The engine ran dynamometer car tests in November 1937 with the result that, although an adequate smokebox vacuum could be maintained with a low exhaust pressure, the excessive fire throwing was a definite disadvantage which led to the removal of the double blast apparatus in 1938. The LMS adopted the simple double blastpipe without the additional petticoat pipes of the Kylchap. This was used on a number of Jubilee class engines. It was observed on No 5553 in 1940 and the double chimney had a period of distinguished service on No 45742 on the Birmingham services in the mid-1950s. The double chimney was removed from No 45742 in 1955 and it survives in preservation on No 5596 *Bahamas*.

No 45584 *North West Frontier* gave the appearance of having two domes owing to the retention of the original top feed casing when given a domed boiler. All the Jubilees shopped at St Rollox had this treatment but in later years it was removed.

Originally there were two types of Jubilee chimney, both with flared sides, the majority being of the shorter pattern. Later a standard pattern emerged as high as the taller original but narrower and with straighter sides. At least one had a squat Black Five chimney and, after 1951 several had the BR standard chimney.

MECHANICAL MODIFICATIONS
LOCO PILOT VALVE

Engine No 5654 *Hood* was fitted with an American type speedometer which gave an indication in the cab of the correct cut off for every speed. An account of the working of such a device on a Niagara class 4-8-4 of the New York Central was given in the April 1952

Issue of *Trains Illustrated* in an article by Dr W. A. Tuplin describing a footplate run on one of these giants. The Jubilee No 5654 with the device ran dynamometer car tests on the Midland XL timings in January 1939. The results showed that, as originally set, the engine run, according to the indication, would not keep time on the up grades but when this was corrected the tendency was to gain time downhill. This is not surprising as the policy of British timetable compilers had always been to discourage fast downhill running. There was a small gain in coal consumption when the engine was driven on the pilot valve but it was not considered sufficient to justify a large scale adoption of the device. It would seem that the device worked better on the "Water Level Route" of the New York Central than on the undulations of the Midland main line. The tests gave some indirect indication of the difficulty of the Midland XL bookings as the calculated ihp needed for time-keeping was 1,605 at Sharnbrook Summit and 1,490 on the climb from Bedford to Luton. A photograph of No 5654 with the apparatus shows that the nameplate was partially obscured but the short name could still be read.

ASH DISPOSAL DEVICES

An ash disposal chute was fitted to engine No 5698 in 1939. The chute extended from the front of the smokebox to a point just to the left of the centre of the front buffer beam. Similar but slightly different variations of the device were noted on No 5702 in 1943 and on 5671 in 1942. The problem of ash accumulation in the smokebox became more acute as the quality of coal declined and as engines were worked harder on long continuous rosters. The various forms of apparatus can hardly have given complete satisfaction as the device was not extended to other members of the class. Any device that made another possible source of leakage in the smokebox of a class of engine that had a reputation for erratic steaming would hardly commend itself to the practical men who had to bear the heat and burden of the day.

TROFINOFF AUTOMATIC BYE PASS VALVES

The Trofinoff Automatic Bye Pass Valve was of Russian origin and it aimed at providing easier coasting when steam was shut off. The valves were tested against ordinary piston valves on Jubilee class engine No 5606 *Falkland Islands* and dynamometer car tests were run between Crewe and Carlisle. The TAB valves allowed the engine to run very freely downhill but the trials did not lead to further large scale use on the LMS. These valves were used on a number of LNER 4-4-0 engines of the GCR Director class and these engines had a good reputation with the men.

REBUILT ENGINES AND UNFULFILLED PROJECTS

Platform end rumour both before and after the building of the first Jubilee suggested that a four-cylinder version was under consideration. This may have been a suggestion but it clearly did not make much progress as there is no mention of such an engine among E. S. Cox's collection of drawings of proposed LMS designs given in his various books. E. S. Cox, however, does reveal that a two-cylinder version was planned in 1937. The idea was that the weight saved by the loss of one cylinder would allow for the use of a larger taper boiler. In 1942 this boiler was actually used with the three cylinders on engines No 5735/6 and this pair became the prototypes for the eventual rebuilding of all the Royal Scots and some of the Patriots.

In the very early days of the Stanier régime it was probable that the Jubilees would have a smaller mixed traffic version in the form of a three-cylinder Class 5 4-6-0. This smaller 4-6-0 would have been the LMS equivalent of the two V4 2-6-2s on the LNER, the last design built by the late Sir Nigel Gresley. The advantage of such an engine, over the two-cylinder 4-6-0s actually built, would have been less hammer blow on the track but against that the reduced accessibility would have increased maintenance costs. The general trend in design during the last twenty years of steam was towards greater simplicity.

In May 1939 the suggestion was made that two purely experimental engines, either of the 5XP or Class 5 Mixed traffic type, should have been fitted with experimental boilers with pressures of up to 300lb/sq in and steam temperatures of up to 750deg F. The smokebox and front end was to allow of various experimental variations and similar variations of cylinder and valve ratios were to be made.

The war brought this interesting idea to a sudden end and there were suggestions after the war the the project should be revived but shortage of money prevented the extension of an idea that might have shortened the time for a test plant to arrive at the truths which governed the basic principles of steam engine design.

TENDERS

Official photographs posed at Crewe Works when the first 5552 was newly built showed her paired with a new type of tender not seen before on LMS engines. It was narrow, flush sided and as high as the cab side sheets with two horizontal lining panels after the style of Fowler tenders. There is no evidence to show that 5552 ever worked in service with this tender and it is authenticated that it ran with 5607 and later with 5609. No 5552 was observed in traffic with a Fowler tender having coal rails, as were the following four engines of the class.

Coupling the engines to the narrow tenders did nothing to enhance their appearance. It seemed as if the drawing office had considered their task complete at the cabside handrails. It was, however, merely a matter of expediency for the tenders were built in advance for some "Baby Scots" which failed to materialise. Contemporary Jubilees were appearing from Glasgow with Stanier high-sided 4,000 gallon tenders built to the full width with curved in tops after trans-Atlantic practice. To add to the confusion there were also some Stanier 3,500 gallon tenders built to the full width but slightly shorter. The difference could be spotted by the position of the horizontal row of rivets at the extreme ends but it is not always easy to identify them from photographs. There was sometimes a more serious confusion on the footplate when using water troughs, both types had similar tender water gauges and unless the fireman had made quite sure that he really had a 4,000 gallon tender there could be uncomfortable results. A hard worked Jubilee could give a fireman a wet shirt quite apart from any external application of water.

In 1936 some of the higher capacity tenders were considered to be of more use on Royal Scots and some Jubilees exchanged tenders with the larger 4–6–0s while some tenders intended for Jubilees went straight to the Royal Scots and the new Jubilees got the Fowler tenders. Such is the force of association that many people thought the Royal Scots looked strange with tenders that were really more in keeping with their size but the Jubilees never looked right with the narrow Fowler tenders.

A glorious game was played with the tenders of the two 5552s. The original 5552 was photographed for its press release in April 1934 with a Stanier high sided narrow tender but it entered service with a Fowler tender. When it was renumbered 5642 it retained its Fowler tender. The original 5642 had a 3,500 gallon tender but it exchanged with the 4,000 gallon tender off 5559 when it was re-numbered 5552 and given its special livery. No 5559 later took the Fowler tender off 5642 in exchange for the 3,500 gallon tender which had originally belonged to the original 5642 which was now 5552.

There were ten of the flush sided tenders built and they were allocated to 5607 to 5616 but apart from the original one, with its unique lining out, they were lined out in a single panel following the contour of the side sheets. It is believed that the intention was to equip 97 of the class with 3,500 gallon tenders and the remaining 94 with 4,000 gallon tenders. These included the fifty locomotives built by the North British Locomotive Company but a report in 1936 showed that, because of the exchange with Royal Scots only 55 of the Jubilees were then fitted with the 4,000 gallon version. An analysis of the tender position was published in the railway press in 1936 but it was never correct in practice. No 5552 was shown as having a 3,500 gallon tender when it already had a 4,000 gallon one with special livery. Not all the class were built when the table was published and there were further exchanges within the class, Nos 5679 and 5740 for example had Royal Scot tenders when built. When new 4,000 gallon tenders with 10 tons of coal capacity were built for the Pacifics in 1936 six of the original Pacific tenders, 4,000 gallons and 9 tons of coal, went to some of the last batch of Jubilees. It is believed that the following table, which is different from the table of intended tender allocations, is correct for 1936:

3500 gallon Fowler ex-compound tender	5553-6/9	
3500 gallon Fowler ex Royal Scot tenders	5557/61–74/85–5606/79–	
	5695–5725/40	70
3500 gallon Fowler ex-compound tender	5560	1
3500 gallon Stanier straight sided	5607–16	10
3500 gallon Stanier curved sided	5617–66	50
4000 gallon Stanier curved sided	5552/8/75–84/5667–78	
	5680–94/5728–37	49
4000 gallon Stanier ex-Princess curved sided tenders	5726/7/38/9/41/2	6

The odd transfer from compound No 1058 was of a spare Fowler tender which went to 5560.

Further changes took place in 1937 when Crewe commenced building fifteen all welded 4,000 gallon tenders similar to those constructed by Armstrong Whitworth for their batches of Black Fives. The first such tender went to 5567 in place of an ex-Royal Scot tender. The replaced Royal Scot tenders went to a new batch of Class 4F 0–6–0s. In 1942 Derby commenced a new batch of forty five 4F 0–6–0s and their tenders were supplied from Jubilees which in turn received new 4,000 gallon tenders. Seven of the ten Stanier straight sided tenders went to 4Fs. The remainder had the already second hand Fowler tenders, 37 of which had originally been on Royal Scots. Of the remaining straight sided tenders 5616 lost hers shortly after nationalisation to an unrebuilt Patriot 45550 but in 1957 the tender found its way back to another Jubilee, this time No 45719. No 5612 and 5613 retained their original tenders for a considerable time until 45612 relinquished hers, in 1959, to 45568 and that from 45613 became the property of another Patriot No 45551 in 1960.

In 1958 it was decreed that all Jubilees were to be fitted with the curved sided tender when they passed through the shops and now it was the turn of the 8F 2-8-0s to be involved in the exchange. No 45704 was the last Jubilee to relinquish its Fowler tender, as late as 1964. Thus another class with non standard tenders was created and 8Fs were to be seen with ex-Royal Scot tenders which had come to them via Jubilee and 4F class engines, while some had acquired the Stanier straight sides from 4Fs.

It is doubtful whether any locomotive in the class ever stayed married to its original tender throughout its existence because they went their separate ways at overhauls. It was not unknown for swaps to be made at the motive power depots and one locomotive inspector remembers starting a week's work on a Jubilee with a high sided tender and finishing with a small one. Some day a more industrious historian may unravel the story in more detail than has been possible in this outline but the fact that Jubilee tenders came from seven different sources shows that interest does not cease at the cab end.

APPEARANCE

Whatever else may be said about the Jubilees it is certain that, in the eyes of the majority, they were not among the most handsome locomotives ever to be designed. Nevertheless they did have a personality of their own being purposeful and businesslike looking machines, somewhat thrusting perhaps, thus lending them the air of sturdy warriors.

LIVERIES

Locomotive livery is a very contentious subject. Many books have been written in detail, their contents culled from a wide field of research but despite this, fierce argument still rages in some quarters as to what was correct. It is said that there are slight variations in the colour vision of most people with "normal" eyesight and even if there could be agreement on the basic colours there were so many variations between the numerous workshops' code of practice and the whims of individuals that it is well nigh impossible to be dogmatic. Generalisation is a safer policy and so let it be with the Jubilees that probably saw as many changes of livery as any class of locomotive.

When first turned out the LMS express passenger livery was still the famous Crimson Lake lined out in yellow with a black edging.

To the LMS enthusiast this was the finest adornment used on any locomotive and its subsequent supplanting by black or green was never really acceptable. However, apart from preserved ex-LMS engines, there are still quite a number of humble NCB tank engines in the area around Leeds that sport the colour and add a touch of warmth among their drab surroundings.

Returning to the Jubilees, those built in 1934/5 and the first part of 1936 carried scroll and serif type numerals normally 12in high in metallic gold, shaded in black, on the cab side approximately in line with the raised running plate and with the power classification 5XP, 2in high, just below the cab windows. The letters LMS were of matching style and colour, 14in high, placed approximately half way up the tender and widely spaced. There were isolated instances of the letters being more closely spaced. Smokebox number plates had 4½in raised scroll type numerals painted white. It is said that while Derby favoured transfers Crewe normally hand painted the insignia.

No 5642 ran for some four months in this livery before being recalled to the paintshop for transfiguration to No 5552 *Silver Jubilee*. The basic colour was "glossy" black with all fittings in polished chromium plate including the outside steam pipes, top feed cover, boiler bands, hand rails, reversing rod, front number block numerals, smokebox door straps and raised cabside numerals and tender lettering. These two latter were of a block sans serif face believed to be the first departure made from the traditional Midland style. No 5552 in this guise survived the war years and almost four years of nationalisation.

Early in 1936 a change from this type face for letters and numerals, including front number blocks, was announced, but it was not until July of that year that this became apparent on the new construction of Jubilees commencing at 5713 to the end of the class. The style was a bold sans serif face, often wrongly described as Gill Sans, again gold shaded red but the numerals were reduced to 10in in height. At this time the lining was changed to chrome yellow. Many of the earlier Jubilees, built in 1934, acquired this style of insignia as they went through shops during the period, except at St Rollox where 10in numerals were applied but they were of the Roman serif pattern shaded black. 5596 has been restored to LMS livery in the St Rollox style. Sans serif was not a popular style and was withdrawn in January 1938 in favour of the old type of insignia which now underwent a change, but of colour only, being in chrome yellow with vermilion red shading. Although there were no more Jubilees to be built those requiring a repaint did receive this treatment as they went through the shops.

Apart from the two standard colours for insignia, of 1928 and 1938, there was one departure, that is gold letters and numerals with red countershading blending to dark red generally applied at Derby after 1929 on black passenger and mixed traffic engines but sometimes transferred on to red locomotives. This particular variation disappeared when the 1938 livery became standard and it is known that some of the Jubilees received this style. Certainly No 5593 can now be seen at Tyseley under preservation with characters of this pleasing appearance.

Wartime brought with it gloom and austerity in almost everything and it was not surprising that from 1940 onwards the familiar colourful liveries were ousted by sombre black. However orders were issued that full repainting was to be undertaken only when really necessary, otherwise patching up was to be carried out. There were a few Jubilees which technically survived the whole six years in red although wartime grime made whatever colour they might once have been a somewhat doubtful quality. That such a thing could have happened at all was however a tribute to the original workmanship and materials. The majority of the class found themselves in unlined black with either plain yellow painted "goods" insignia or with yellow shaded red transfers. In many cases the workshops or even motive power depots merely freshened up the paintwork of the numerals and letters so that many curious hues were in evidence.

With the cessation of hostilities it was assumed that conditions would return to normal but this turned out to be wishful thinking for the funereal black seemed to have entered the soul of the LMS and there it was to remain, with small concessions to enlivement, as a standard policy after experiments were carried out with other colours. Two of the Jubilee class were chosen as the guinea pigs and neither of them, in the event, proved very spectacular.

No 5573 was outshopped early in 1946 in a slate blue-grey livery lined out in golden yellow with crimson outer edging. The insignia was in yellow 12in sans serif style and unshaded.

The other locomotive of the class, No 5594, appeared at the same time in a dark shade of maroon, not crimson lake as sometimes supposed, lined out in yellow edged black, except for the splashers, with the same type face for the insignia as on 5573.

It is evident that neither of these two unbecoming styles of painting found favour for almost immediately the next standard livery was announced. Express passenger locomotives, including the Jubilees, were to be painted black with a lining of maroon having a narrow line of straw colour on either side flanked with black outer edges. The insignia was to be 12in high bold block "straw" numerals, unshaded but outlined in maroon and straw all round. The tender letters were similar but 14in high. Lining to boiler barrels and the maroon lining to the insignia was absent in the initial stages. Name-plates were to be maroon backed. One particularly pleasing feature was that running numbers were to be raised to a position below the cab windows bringing them into line with the LMS on the tender, while the power classification 5XP was featured lower on the cabside. When new from the paintshop this particular livery was not un-pleasing but it was unpopular with enthusiasts. Possibly the LMS authorities were wise in accepting the fact that man-power shortage in the postwar world meant that whatever colour was intended, it would in a few weeks be indistinguishable under a layer of grime.

Owing to the short period of time between the decision on the new livery and the nationalisation of the railways, in January 1948, not all of the Jubilees were running in these colours when the new regime commenced. There were still at least fourteen of the class in red, including the maroon 5594, of which several became renumbered in the 40000 series while retaining the original LMS colour and tender letters.

Once again there was a period of upheaval and for a few years Jubilees presented a most hybrid appearance. Immediately following nationalisation temporary expedients were put into practice. The first of these was to put the words British Railways in full on the tender in a plain block style more akin to Gill Saɑs than previously and again officially it was in straw colour but whereas LMS straw was a pale yellow, almost cream, BR straw was cream, almost off white! Until the renumbering scheme was finalised regional letters were appended to the running numbers. Thus on the London Midland region, formerly the LMS, locomotives received a painted letter M below the numerals on the cabside and a metal plate with raised M painted white was welded as a prefix to the front number block. The basic colour varied from residual red, through plain black to lined black but many ran for several years still retaining the letters LMS on their tenders. It was not unknown for red locomotives to have black tenders and vice versa during the 1940s.

The new British Railways were as uncertain as the LMS had been two years previously as to what standard livery should be adopted and again selected engines were the subject of experimental colours. Among locomotives of other classes there were three Jubilees painted in a light green, sometimes described as apple green but certainly not as bright as the LNER green, fully lined out in red, grey and black with pale straw insignia. The characters are believed to have been 10in high with British Railways still in full.The new numbering now in force gave most of the former LMS locomotives an added 40000 to their original numbers. Nos 45565, 45604 and 45694 were the engines in question and the front number blocks on 45565 and 45694 were cast with the numerals in sans serif face; a reversion to the 1936 style. The position of the lining out was not in accordance with LMS practice and was brought a few inches in from the edges of the tender and cab sides.

A further temporary livery, later adopted for mixed traffic and smaller passenger locomotives, was given a trial on 45709 and at least 10 others but this was a familiar livery of pre-grouping days being that of the former LNWR. It is believed that this was carried out at Crewe and no doubt gave satisfaction to some old timers who, remembering the Nor'Western engines suffering the "indignity" of Midland red in the 1920s, got their revenge when they saw a Fowler tender decked out in Webb colours!

However it was not LNER green, nor LMS black, nor LNWR black that was finally chosen as the BR standard express livery but GWR Brunswick green with GWR type black/orange/black lining. Sans serif numerals were standardised in the off-white shade but only 8in high while the large lion and wheel emblem was applied to the tender. Vermilion backed nameplates were the order of the day to the vociferous discontent of many who had forgotten that this practice had been standard on the Southern Railway and no one had complained. St Rollox however, always radical, went their own way and applied numerals at least 12in high to Jubilees, and other classes, repainted therein.

This general livery remained with the Jubilees until the end except for the change to a smaller and more decorative emblem in 1957. *Silver Jubilee* herself lost the distinctive black livery in 1951 and became green along with the rest but with the concession of chrome raised numerals 45552.

In the declining days of steam it was not considered economic to give full repainting to locomotives of short life expectancy so many, including a few Jubilees, finished their days in unlined green. With the overhead electrification of the West Coast main line certain classes were banned south of Crewe from September 1964. The Jubilees still in traffic were among those chosen and to remind engine crews a 5in yellow stripe was painted diagonally below the cab windows. It is however certain that many of the Jubilees still officially in stock were in storage and so escaped the treatment.

Minor detailed differences in insignia were brought about when the 5XP engines were uprated to Class 6P in 1951 and further to 6P5F late in 1955 but it is doubtful if the latter classification was ever painted on the locomotives themselves.

When the foregoing liveries are permutated with the various combinations of tenders, chimneys and boiler outlines one is tempted to wonder if there ever was such a thing as a typical Jubilee.

ALLOCATIONS

As we have seen from earlier chapters the Jubilee class was designed as a second line express engine and at first they were allocated to the appropriate sheds. On the Midland the pre-grouping policy of short out and back runs was still in practice when the Jubilees entered the scene. By 1938 engine changing on the principal expresses was a thing of the past at such places as Derby, Nottingham and Leicester. To obtain maximum availability six or seven day rosters ensured that locomotives were kept on the move as much as possible but not always on the work for which they were designed nor, at times, on work which suited them. An engine might return to its home shed after being through the hands of up to a dozen different engine crews and having seen service at the head of fast expresses, stopping trains, fitted freight or, during the war, loose coupled mineral trains. If a failure took place and a substitute had to take over, engines strayed far from their normal territory, all of this was not good for the engines but it brought joy to the lineside spotter who never quite knew what rare engine would turn up. At some stations Jubilees were employed as main line pilots dutifully shunting empty stock or milk tanks but ready all the time for the call to take over an express that was in trouble, either alone or as pilot engine.

With the advent of main line diesel locomotives the Jubilees, along with many other classes, were gradually displaced from their normal activities and were dispersed to other depots where useful but less strenuous work could be performed. Many of these duties were mundane and menial such as local pick-up goods workings and even coal trains. They were seen more frequently on lines where previously they had only worked in a desultory fashion such as the GCR south of Sheffield.

During the course of their existence the Jubilees were spread round to at least 60 motive power depots but in their heyday less than half this number were involved. It is difficult to pinpoint exactly how many new engines were allocated to each particular depot as many were officially designated as Crewe North but this was merely for running-in purposes before moving off to another depot. It is perhaps surprising that after 20 years the whole of the class were basically still at the same depots though not in the same quantities nor with the same individual engines. This does not mean that in the interim other depots were not involved, for during the war several Jubilees went to unusual depots not normally associated with passenger engines. Seasonal transfers also took place during the summer timetables which are now merely a memory. It may be asked if any of the Jubilees remained at one depot throughout the whole of their existence as has been known with other locomotives? The answer is a conjectural "yes" because during the war years regular transfer lists were not always available but despite this it is believed that No 5659 was always at Leeds (Holbeck) and 5701 similarly stayed faithful to Newton Heath (Manchester).

It is felt that a balanced picture of the typical geographical deployment of the class can best be given by listing the quantity of Jubilees stationed at the various depots concerned at January 1, 1938 when they had at last settled into routine and at January 1, 1958 before displacement by diesels and large scale scrapping had set in. However it may be well to note firstly the sheds to which Jubilees were originally sent when brand new. These were:

Willesden	Chester	Upperby	Southport
Camden	Holyhead	Kentish Town	Blackpool
Rugby	Edge Hill	Derby	Low Moor
Bushbury	Longsight	Millhouses	Farnley Junc
Aston	Preston	Holbeck	Newton Heath
Crewe North	Durran Hill	Bristol	

Number of Jubilees allocated to basic depots at given dates:

	1/1/38	1/1/58		1/1/38	1/1/58
Willesden	4	2	Kentish Town	19	10
Camden	5	9	Nottingham	3	6
Rugby	10	nil	Derby	7	3
Bushbury	nil	10	Millhouses	6	12
Crewe North	33	19	Holbeck	14	18
Holyhead	4	nil	Bristol	nil	10
Edge Hill	4	8	Blackpool	7	6
Longsight	6	11	Newton Heath	9	8
Preston	9	2	Bank Hall	nil	3
Patricroft	6	6	Polmadie	1	2
Kingmoor	15	18	Corkerhill	2	6
Upperby	12	7	St Rollox	1	nil
Farnley Junc	8	4	Perth	2	3
Trafford Park	nil	7	Aberdeen	4	nil

The difference in the engine totals is accounted for by the withdrawal of 45637 in 1952 after the Harrow accident.

In 1938, despite the improved test results of Jubilees in 1937, the Patriots were still working the Euston–Wolverhampton trains hence there were no Jubilees allocated to Bushbury but there was a large scale transfer in March 1939. In 1938 Derby was responsible for the West of England workings with no Jubilees stationed at Bristol shed. The Jubilee class was banned from Manchester Central prior to June 1938 on account of bridge strengthening being undertaken on the approaches to the station. After June 1938 Jubilees were stationed at Trafford Park depot and the permitted loads over Peak Forest were increased from 255 tons for Class 5 to 275 tons for Class 5XP on the XL timings.

During the LMS régime Jubilees were allocated at various periods for varying lengths of time to the following additional depots:

Bescot	Saltley	Bangor	Normanton
Walsall	Shrewsbury	Carnforth	Accrington
Monument Lane	Llandudno	Grimesthorpe	

After nationalisation they also saw service from:

Chester (WR)	Warrington	Burton	Neasden (GC)
Nuneaton	Speke Junc	Canklow	Annesley (GC)
Crewe South	Stockport	Agecroft	Darnall (GC)
Birkenhead	Leicester	Wakefield	

It is believed that the largest Jubilee influx ever known to one depot in a single batch was in December 1961 when Burton-on-Trent found itself with 18 newcomers.

It would appear that, apart from early period on loan to Midland division sheds to show itself, *Silver Jubilee* worked solely on the West Coast route, mainly from Preston, Edgehill and Crewe North and after an early spell at Holbeck for trial running to Glasgow the two rebuilt engines did likewise. However No 45736 finished at Kingmoor and 45735, after an undistinguished short career on the Great Central, made its exit from, of all places, Annesley.

In 1952 there was a large scale transfer to ensure that the Scottish area engines were those with 31sq ft grates. The boilers with 29·5sq ft grates were not interchangeable. The intention was to simplify repair work by having all the Scottish area engines of one type. There were more engines with 31sq ft grate area than were needed in Scotland so, although all Scottish engines had the larger grates, all the larger grates were not in Scotland.

Holbeck depot, Leeds, hung tenaciously to a few remaining Jubilees right up to the end, the last one being 45562 which was withdrawn from that depot. Of the eight remaining in stock during

No 45735 *Comet,* rebuilt with larger
boiler, leaving Eccles with a
Manchester-Barrow train in June 1959.
[W. Cooper

**A CLASS 7
REBUILD**

No 45739 *Ulster* on return party special from Co to Bradford at Meash on July 15, 1963. [G.

Shorn of most of its silver trimmings No 45552 has them restored by nature while in store in the great frost of 1963. [D. Wignall

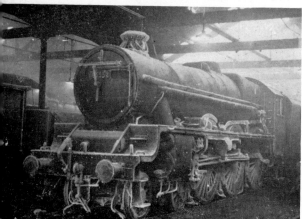

No 45675 *Hardy* and an Austerity 2–8–0 on a Heysham-Leeds oil train at Giggleswick on May 20, 1967. [S. James

?ILEE
LLANY

᠎593 *Kolhapur* entering Appleby with the 10.17am Leeds-Glasgow express on July 15, 1967. [T. G. Hepburn

No 45662 *Kempenfelt* passing Southampton Central with the 2.20pm Fawley-Bromford Bridge oil train on September 21, 1961. [J. C. Haydon

A Jubilee on the Met! No 45709 *Implacable* at Amersham with the Centenary Special from Aylesbury on May 26, 1961. [E. J. S. Gadsen

No 5593 *Kolhapur* preserved by Clun Castle Ltd at its new home at Tyseley. [Ivo Peters

No 5596 *Bahamas* at Stockport Edgeley mpd before transfer to Dinting for preservation by Bahamas Locomotive Society [Brian Stephenson

JUBILEES IN PRESERVATION

the final year, 1967, six were allocated to Holbeck and two to Wakefield, both former Leeds engines.

LOAD LIMITS

The classification 5XP was first used by the LMS to distinguish the Claughtons rebuilt with the larger boiler from the rest of Class 5. It was continued for the Patriots which had the same boiler and for the Jubilees developed from the Patriots. In the early days of nationalisation it was decided to uprate Class 5X engines to Class 6 and Classes 6 and 7 to 7 and 8. The Jubilees became Class 6 and the two large boilered rebuilds Class 7. In prewar days the LMS kept rather more rigidly to their limit loads than the GWR and more especially, the LNER south of York.

Class 6 load limits

	Full load	Limited load	Special limit	XL limit
LNWR main line				
Euston to Carnforth	495 tons	430 tons	390 tons	350 tons
Carnforth to Carlisle	415 tons	365 tons	285 tons	
Midland main line ..				
Derby to Leicester	470 tons	415 tons	375 tons	300 tons
Nottingham – St Pancras ..				
Leicester – St Pancras ..	440 tons	390 tons	350 tons	300 tons
GCR main line				
Marylebone–Woodford				
via Aylesbury	390 tons	350 tons		
Marylebone–Woodford				
via High Wycombe ..	415 tons	375 tons		
Woodford–Nottingham ..	415 tons	375 tons		
Nottingham–Sheffield ..	400 tons	350 tons		

The XL limit of 300 tons applied to the very fast Midland timings generally introduced in 1957. The load limit was just exceeded by 9 bogies of BR stock and at first there was usually some slight tolerance but I have photographs and logs where the pilot was called for 9 bogies, doubtless in some cases when there were doubts about the steaming of the train engine. The Jubilee on the 8.33 from Leicester to St Pancras from September 1957 was regularly piloted by a Class 5 which was needed for a return working.

UNUSUAL AND SPECIAL WORKINGS

During the first half of their lives the Jubilees kept reasonably close to their intended work, although they could occasionally be seen on branch lines such as Leicester-Rugby, but after nationalisation they turned up in odd places and under strange circumstances. Before the war they took a share in the working of Royal Trains, in pairs on the heavy night train, as had been the case with Claughtons in the 1920s. Only a Pacific was considered capable of managing such a load unassisted with reliability. In 1937 Nos 5741 and 5742 took the Royal Special to Aintree while Nos 5589 and 5603, 5670 and 5678 were noted on Royal Trains in 1938. In the troubled months before World War II Nos 5686 and 5692 were noted together and on a shorter journey with a lighter train No 5674 managed alone. After the war No M5606 was noted on a Royal special to Birmingham in May 1948. When the Prime Minister, then Winston Churchill, returned from his momentous visit to America in 1942 his special train from Liverpool to Euston was hauled by No 5593 *Kolhapur* which survives in preservation.

The war years brought about some hitherto quite unthinkable duties to the Jubilees, some of which were not without their humerous appeal. In 1942 a coal train with an ex-LNWR 0–8–0 at the head was banked in the rear past Bescot by Jubilee No 5603. A heavy troop train was noted between Nuneaton and Wigston with a Jubilee piloted by a 0–8–0. Perhaps the queerest example of piloting took place when, in 1942, a Stroudley D1 class 0–4–2T, which was at Ayr for station pilot duties, was called out as assistant engine to a Jubilee once to Girvan and once to Glenwhilly.

Jubilees ranged far and wide on specials especially during the 1960s. In the West Country Jubilees penetrated as far as Exeter and Goodrington and also to Weston-super-Mare, Swansea and Weymouth. March once sent No 45669 on a freight train to Cambridge. In 1950 they were rostered on a Newcastle through working and for many years they worked into York, while on holiday specials they made their way to Bridlington, Saltburn, Hull, Scarborough and Skegness. At least one visited Kings Cross when 45597 worked up on an excursion from Bradford.

It was on the Southern Region that they lived most dangerously for on several occasions they were arrested for wrongful entry. They had been seen on the LSWR at such places as Eastleigh, Fawley and Southampton on pigeon specials or on oil tank trains but the Brighton line shunned them. The first recorded visit was in 1953 when No 45595 reached Brighton and returned unmolested but in 1961 a Leicester to Brighton day excursion caused a furore as No 45650 *Blake* was not allowed to take the return working and a Schools was substituted. *Blake* sneaked back light engine a fortnight later. Next year the LMR tried another admiral, *Anson*, not to Brighton but on the Newhaven Car Sleeper train. *Anson* had the misfortune to fail at Lewes on the return trip and so gave its presence away and was taken into custody at Brighton. The next day No 45617 got to Newhaven but on being sent to Eastbourne shed for servicing she also was arrested. After nearly two weeks the two trespassers were sent home with a warning not to exceed 25mph and not to do it again.

It may be claimed that over perhaps 75per cent of the railway system of Great Britain at one time or another the voice of the Jubilee has been heard in the land.

MILEAGE AND AVAILABILITY

One of the aims of the designer had been to obtain much greater mileage and availability from the Jubilee class as compared with the older classes that they replaced. To this end long cyclic workings were introduced and these have been criticised in some quarters as being too exacting for the engines to work with reliability. It has always been the case with both the steam engine and now with the diesel that the targets for mileage and availability have been over optimistic. A comparison with other contemporary classes of steam engines forms a better yardstick. Some evidence of the mileage and availability of the Jubilee class comes from a table published in the December 1957 issue of *Trains Illustrated*. The availability of the leading LMR express engines between January 1 and September 30, 1957 was given as follows:

Loco	Days in works	Days on Shed	Days worked	Mileage
BR Class 8 4–6–2 No 71000 ..	24	58	148	39709
LMR Coronation Class 4–6–2	30	41	159	56800
BR Britannia class 4–6–2 ..	30	42	160	43158
LMR Royal Scot class 4–6–0	35	45	150	41314
LMR Jubilee class 4–6–0 ..	22	41	167	45503

The Jubilee shows up very well in this comparison taking second place only in average mileage behind the larger Coronation class Pacific. Some confirmation of these figures comes from mileage figures of three Jubilee class engines taken at random, these worked out at 1,338,515 and 1,482,321 for two engines which had run for 25 years and an excellent 1,384,000 for 22 years. This suggests that the average annual mileage worked out at 50–60,000 miles per annum, slightly less than the best of the LMS and LNER Pacifics but a figure roughly comparable with the best of contemporary 4–6–0s such as the GWR Castles.

ACCIDENTS

Accidents are not a cheerful subject and the number of Jubilee casualties was not excessive in relation to the mileage worked. No serious accident took place because of any proved deficiencies of basic design. They had a reputation for better riding and fewer

frame fractures than most LMR 4–6–0s. Unfortunately a Jubilee
was involved in one of the worst of British accidents and after the
terrible multiple collision at Harrow in 1952, which was excelled
in horror only by Quintinstill, No 45637 *Windward Islands* was
withdrawn. After a freight train accident in 1961, when No 45630
was in collision with Class 5 No 45401, both engines were withdrawn but this was a matter of policy because it had been decreed
that no more money was to be spent on steam engine repairs. A few
years earlier both engines would have been repaired.

PRESERVATION

At one time it was hoped to preserve No 5660 *Rooke* because of its
record hill climbing performances on the test trains of October 1937
but this proved to be impossible. Nevertheless it is good to be able
to report the survival of No 5593 *Kolhapur* at Tyseley in the hands of
Clun Castle Ltd and the double chimneyed No 5596 *Bahamas*
preserved by Bahamas Locomotive Society at Dinting Junction. Both
engines have been restored to a state of resplendent well-being
that reflects the greatest credit on their owners.

NAMES

When the taper boilered 5XP class first appeared their lack of names
was bitter disappointment to youthful eyes. It was expected that the
tradition of naming express engines would be perpetuated. The
convention was to say that locomotives were "honoured" with names
but it is straining credulity to suggest that some of the clumsy and
unsuitable names foisted on innocent locomotives were an honour.
The addition of a name was, however, in present day terms a status
symbol which doubtless created the desired effect on the public at
large. To the average railway enthusiast a name gave pleasure and
an added touch of glamour to lineside observation.

In the 1930s Britain was not ashamed of its Empire nor of its armed
forces and the LMS had been rather aggressively nationalistic in its
choice of names with royal ladies and regiments giving names to
Pacifics and Royal Scots. This was in contrast to the more sporting
flavour of LNER names with race horses, football teams and packs
of hounds appearing on locomotive name plates. It was fully in the
LMS tradition that they decided to commemorate the Silver Jubilee
of their Majesties King George V and Queen Mary in May 1935 by
naming an engine *Silver Jubilee* and giving it a uniquely distinguished
livery. This caused rejoicing among the young locomotive fans of the
day.

The locomotive chosen was not a new one but No 5642 built at Crewe in November 1934 and popularly supposed to be "the best of the bunch". There was a direct change of numbers between two locomotives, 5642 becoming *Silver Jubilee* and 5552 taking the identity of 5642 complete with small Fowler tender. Thus the Red Staniers, the Claughton Replacements or the Tapered 5XPs or whatever clumsy description was used became known as the Silver Jubilee class but in the typically British fashion of abbreviating everything possible they were soon just Jubilees. In the trendy post-war years the juvenile spotters pruned this down to the ugly connotation "Jubes" but this is best forgotten.

Silver Jubilee was sent on temporary loan to several motive power depots in all parts of the system to "show the flag" before settling down to life at Preston.

Later in December of the same year, when the new series of modified Jubilees emerged from Crewe the first one carried a name that required a double decker nameplate. No 5665 was named *Lord Rutherford of Nelson* (in New Zealand) who had recently performed the opening ceremony of the LMS Research Laboratory in Derby. It was in keeping with prior arrangements to name certain locomotives after eminent personalities connected with the railways but was it always necessary to use the full title? Multi-word nameplates occupying two lines of capitals always seemed so cumbersome.

Subsequent locomotives continued to enter traffic without names and it was assumed that the *status quo* had been maintained until it was reported that a Jubilee, one of the old ones, had been seen in service with the strange name *Indore*. At the same time visitors to Crewe Works witnessed that newly built locomotives in the 5680 series were having names commemorating sea battles. This was no new innovation for some of these had already been borne many years previously on various LNWR types.

Confusion as to what the policy for naming the Jubilees might be was short lived despite an initial feeling that perhaps only a chosen few might have greatness thrust upon them as was the case with the Patriots. Early in 1936 the railway periodicals were able to publish the list of names which had been selected to grace the class and although the underlying theme was quite sound some of the individual names were a little unpalatable. Taken out of context they could look quite fatuous.

Following *Silver Jubilee* the next 86 locomotives were to be named after British Colonies, Commonwealth countries and dependencies and the various states within. The order of naming was curious for they first commenced in some geographical sequence, with *Canada* and sub-divisions followed by the Antipodes but then *South Africa*, *Irish Free State* and a belated *Newfoundland* found themselves immediately preceding a long list of Indian States with *Southern Rhodesia* bringing up the rear. Then they decided to follow Great Western practice and catalogue the remainder alphabetically but with *Solomon Islands* an odd man out among the Cs.

The next set was of thirty-nine distinguished Admirals, broken by the intrusion of *Lord Rutherford of Nelson* who found himself next to *Nelson*, the victor of Trafalgar. Then there was a short series of eight famous sea battles which was followed by, one submits, the best lot of names since the LNWR held sway, namely warships of the line. *Achilles, Colossus, Thunderer, Express, Swiftsure, Furious* and the like were probably more suited to steam locomotives than to the graceful sailing ships which first bore them. Some of them had of course been repeated by the Navy on vessels of the steam era and what better names could round off the personality of a mighty iron clad monster of the track? These were proud names to be sure, fully in the tradition of LMS patriotism when Britannia really did rule the waves.

Shortly before the Jubilees were built the LMS had renamed 25 Royal Scots, which had been bearing the names of pioneer locomotives of the Stephenson era, to conform with the regimental majority. Eight of the discarded names were selected for the penultimate Jubilees clearing the way for the last four to be named, almost as an afterthought, after the four divisions of Ireland.

One hundred and ninety names in all, many of which were memorable but a few best forgotten. A correspondent in the *Railway Magazine* was quick to point out that the innocent recipient of the name *Tonga* could have been the victim of a malicious humourist for in the East a tonga is a ramshackle two wheeled horse drawn conveyance in which one rides at one's peril! Actually of course *Tonga* was named after the Island whose Queen was such a colourful and popular figure at the 1953 Coronation so the engine's name was probably understood in its latter years.

The nameplates were of the standard LMS radius type of cast brass, concentric with the leading splasher above which they were mounted, with raised polished beading and letters. The background was of black enamel. *Silver Jubilee* of course had chromium plated letters and beading. Letters were of a plain block sans serif style but those plates cast at St Rollox had a less bold type face. In the main the plates were manufactured at Crewe but there were a few cast at Derby or at St Rollox for the locomotives working in Scotland

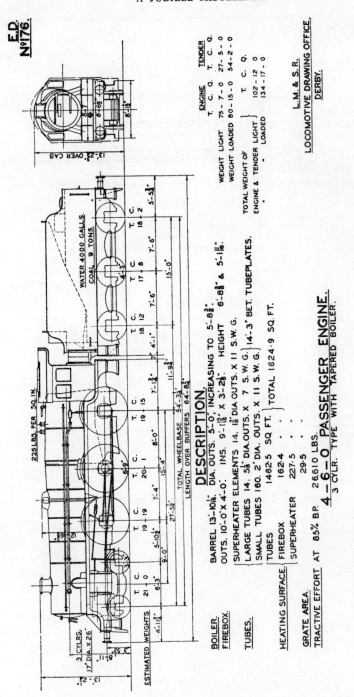

E.D.
Nº176.

WATER 4000 GALLS.
COAL 9 TONS.

ENGINE   TENDER
       T. C. Q.   T. C. Q.
WEIGHT LIGHT   75 - 7 - 0   27 - 5 - 0
WEIGHT LOADED 80 - 15 - 0   54 - 2 - 0

                T. C. Q.
TOTAL WEIGHT OF   102 - 12 - 0
ENGINE & TENDER LIGHT
        LOADED   134 - 17 - 0

L.M.& S.R.
LOCOMOTIVE DRAWING OFFICE,
DERBY.

DESCRIPTION.

BOILER. BARREL 13'-10⅛". DIA. OUTS. 5'-0", INCREASING TO 5'-8⅜".
FIREBOX. OUTS. 10'-0" X 4'-0". INS. 9'-1¹⁵⁄₁₆" X 3'-2⅞". HEIGHT 6'-8½" & 5'-1⅛"

TUBES. SUPERHEATER ELEMENTS 14. 1⅜" DIA OUTS. X 11 S.W. G.
LARGE TUBES 14. 5¼" DIA.OUTS. X 7 S. W. G.) 14'-3" BET. TUBEPLATES.
SMALL TUBES 160. 2" DIA. OUTS. X 11 S.W. G.)

HEATING SURFACE. TUBES 1482·5 SQ FT.) TOTAL 1624·9 SQ. FT.
FIREBOX 162·4 "
SUPERHEATER 227·5 "

GRATE AREA 29·5 "
TRACTIVE EFFORT AT 85% B.P. 26,610 LBS.

4—6—0 PASSENGER ENGINE.
3 CYLR. TYPE WITH TAPERED BOILER.

225 LBS. PER SQ. IN.

3 CYLRS.
17" DIA. x 26"

ESTIMATED WEIGHTS

The LMS Jubilee class 4-6-0 original design.

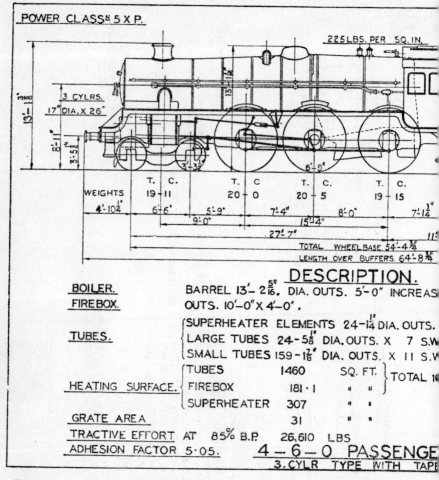

POWER CLASS№ 5 X P.

225 LBS. PER SQ. IN.

3 CYLRS.
17" DIA. X 26"

13' – 1"

8'–1"
3'–5½"

4'–3½"   6'–9"

WEIGHTS	T. C. 19 – 11	T. C 20 – 0	T. C. 20 – 5	T. C. 19 – 15

4'–10¼"   6'–6"   5'–9"   7'–4"   8'–0"   7'–1¼"
9'–0"
15'–4"
27'–7"

TOTAL WHEELBASE 54'–4¾"
LENGTH OVER BUFFERS 64'–8¾"

DESCRIPTION.

BOILER.   BARREL 13'– 2⁵⁄₁₆". DIA. OUTS. 5'–0" INCREAS

FIREBOX.   OUTS. 10'–0" X 4'–0'.

TUBES.   SUPERHEATER ELEMENTS 24–1¼" DIA. OUTS.
          LARGE TUBES 24–5⅜" DIA. OUTS. X 7 S.W
          SMALL TUBES 159–1⅞" DIA. OUTS. X 11 S.W

HEATING SURFACE.   TUBES   1460   SQ. FT.   TOTAL 1
          FIREBOX   181·1   "   "
          SUPERHEATER   307   "   "

GRATE AREA   31   "   "

TRACTIVE EFFORT AT 85% B.P.   26,610   LBS

ADHESION FACTOR 5·05.   4 – 6 – 0 PASSENGE
          3. CYLR TYPE WITH TAPE

The LMS Jubilee class 4-6-0 5xp design with modified boiler.

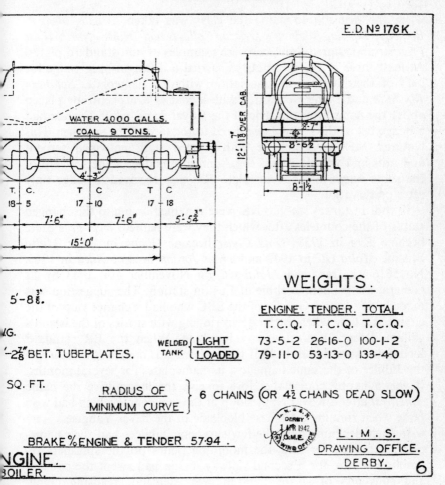

E.D. Nº 176 K.

WATER 4,000 GALLS.
COAL 9 TONS.

12'-11⅛ OVER CAB.   7'

3'-7"
8'-6½"

8'-1½"

4'-3"

T. C.   T   C   T   C
18-5   17-10   17-18

7'-6"   7'-6"   5'-5¾"

15'-0"

5'-8⅜.

NG.

-2⅞" BET. TUBEPLATES.

SQ. FT.

WELDED { LIGHT
TANK { LOADED

WEIGHTS.

	ENGINE.	TENDER.	TOTAL.
	T. C. Q.	T. C. Q.	T. C. Q.
LIGHT	73-5-2	26-16-0	100-1-2
LOADED	79-11-0	53-13-0	133-4-0

RADIUS OF
MINIMUM CURVE } 6 CHAINS (OR 4½ CHAINS DEAD SLOW)

BRAKE % ENGINE & TENDER 57·94 .

NGINE.
BOILER.

L. M. S.
DRAWING OFFICE.
DERBY.   6

L.M.&.R.
DERBY
1 APR 1942
C.M.E.
WING OFFICE

when the decision to name the class was taken. *Assam, Bengal, Bombay, Burma, Bihar and Orissa, Collingwood, Howe, North West Frontier* and *United Provinces* were examples of non-standard plates. At least three of the locomotives carried a distinguishing badge for part of their careers in association with the nameplate. *Southern Rhodesia* and *Ulster* were fitted with a coat of arms centrally placed above the name after the style of the Royal Scots, while *Express* had a badge below the nameplate affixed to the face of the splasher. This featured Mercury complete with winged staff, entwined serpent and sails and was doubtless the Admiralty badge of the warship of the same name. Strange to relate *Bahamas* received a badge only after preservation.

In four instances locomotives were renamed owing to the changed status of the countries after which they were named. *Irish Free State* became *Eire* in 1938; *Gold Coast* became *Ghana* in 1958; *Malta* became *Malta GC* in 1943 and *Trans-Jordan* became *Aden* in 1946. No 5616 was renamed *Malta GC* on November 4th, 1943 by Lt General Sir William Dobbie at Euston station. The suggestion was made by Mr Lionel Gamlin of the BBC who had a chance view of the engine at a time when the land was ringing with stories of the island's gallant defence against enemy bombing. When the BR standard locomotives were built in 1951 the first one was named *Britannia* and the Jubilee of the same name lost its nameplates for several months. It was a happy choice therefore to give the locomotive the name *Amethyst* after a Royal Navy sloop of the same name which had won fame when running a Chinese blockade of the River Yangtse.

In their declining days the few surviving Jubilees had their nameplates removed for sale, the mounting plates on the splashers remaining *in situ*, for a second railway mania had swept the country and souvenirs of steam were in great demand, realising highly inflated purchase prices.

Engine summary

NO	SELECTED NAME 1935/6	REMARKS
5552	*Silver Jubilee*	Formerly 5642, Special livery, named 1935.
5553	*Canada*	Double chimney 1940.
5554	*Ontario*	Test climbs of Lickey Incline Mar 1955.
5555	*Quebec*	
5556	*Nova Scotia*	Used in 1934 dynamometer car trials.
5557	*New Brunswick*	
5558	*Manitoba*	Fast run on up "Royal Scot", Chap 7.
5559	*British Columbia*	
5560	*Prince Edward Island*	
5561	*Saskatchewan*	
5562	*Alberta*	Last of class to be withdrawn 1967.
5563	*Australia*	
5564	*New South Wales*	
5565	*Victoria*	BR experimental livery 1948.
5566	*Queensland*	
5567	*South Australia*	
5568	*Western Australia*	
5569	*Tasmania*	
5570	*New Zealand*	
5571	*South Africa*	
5572	*Irish Free State*	Renamed *Eire*, July 9, 1938.
5573	*Newfoundland*	Experimental blue/grey livery, 1946.
5574	*India*	
5575	*Madras*	
5576	*Bombay*	
5577	*Bengal*	
5578	*United Provinces*	
5579	*Punjab*	Highest authentic Jubilee speed 97½mph at MP 48, Chap 10.
5580	*Burma*	
5581	*Bihar and Orisa*	
5582	*Central Provinces*	
5583	*Assam*	
5584	*North West Frontier*	Original dome shaped casing over top feed retained giving impression of two domes. Chap 12.
5585	*Hyderabad*	High speed test run prior to introduction of Midland Pullman.
5586	*Mysore*	
5587	*Baroda*	
5588	*Kashmir*	

NO	SELECTED NAME 1935/6	REMARKS
5589	Gwalior	Outstanding performer in early 1950s.
5590	Travancore	
5591	Udaipur	
5592	Indore	
5593	Kolhapur	Used on special train Liverpool Euston 1942 on return of the Prime Minister, Mr Winston Churchill, from America. Preserved at Tyseley, 1967.
5594	Bhopal	Experimental maroon livery, 1946.
5595	Southern Rhodesia	Coat of arms above nameplate.
5596	Bahamas	Double chimney 1961. Preserved at Dinting.
5597	Barbados	96mph. Chap 10.
5598	Basutoland	
5599	Bechuanaland	
5600	Bermuda	
5601	British Guiana	Modified draughting 1957.
5602	British Honduras	
5603	Solomon Islands	
5604	Ceylon	BR experimental light green livery, 1948.
5605	Cyprus	
5606	Falkland Islands	Trofinoff Automatic Bye-pass valves, 1938. Modified draughting 1957.
5607	Fiji	
5608	Gibraltar	
5609	Gilbert and Ellice Islands	First to be withdrawn from normal service 1960.
5610	Gold Coast	Renamed Ghana Dec 1958. Modified draughting 1957.
5611	Hong Kong	
5612	Jamaica	
5613	Kenya	
5614	Leeward Islands	Used in high speed trials St Pancras to Leeds, April 1957, Chap 6.
5615	Malay States	
5616	Malta	Renamed Malta GC, Nov 1943.
5617	Mauritius	
5618	New Hebrides	
5619	Nigeria	
5620	North Borneo	
5621	Northern Rhodesia	
5622	Nyasaland	Fastest prewar run Leicester-St Pancras Chap 7. Modified draughting 1957.
5623	Palestine	
5624	St Helena	
5625	Sarawak	
5626	Seychelles	
5627	Sierra Leone	
5628	Somaliland	Modified draughting 1957.
5629	Straits Settlements	
5630	Swaziland	
5631	Tanganyika	

NO	SELECTED NAME 1935/6	REMARKS
5632	*Tonga*	
5633	*Trans Jordan*	Renamed *Aden* Sept 1946.
5634	*Trinidad*	
5635	*Tobago*	
5636	*Uganda*	Fast postwar run Leicester-St Pancras, Chap 10.
5637	*Windward Islands*	Withdrawn after Harrow collision 1952.
5638	*Zanzibar*	
5639	*Raleigh*	
5640	*Frobisher*	
5641	*Sandwich*	
5642	*Boscawen*	Formerly 5552, first to be built 1934.
5643	*Rodney*	
5644	*Howe*	
5645	*Collingwood*	
5646	*Napier*	
5647	*Sturdee*	
5648	*Wemyss*	
5649	*Hawkins*	
5650	*Blake*	
5651	*Shovell*	
5652	*Hawke*	
5653	*Barham*	
5654	*Hood*	Fitted with American speedometer and pilot valve, 1939, 96mph. Chap 10.
5655	*Keith*	
5656	*Cochrane*	
5657	*Tyrwhitt*	
5658	*Keyes*	
5659	*Drake*	Ran in service in pink undercoat, 1955.
5660	*Rooke*	Used in Bristol-Glasgow trial running October, 1937.
5661	*Vernon*	
5662	*Kempenfelt*	
5663	*Jervis*	
5664	*Nelson*	
5665	*Lord Rutherford of Nelson*	First of class to be built with nameplates, 1935. First of new series with redesigned boiler.
5666	*Cornwallis*	
5667	*Jellicoe*	
5668	*Madden*	
5669	*Fisher*	
5670	*Howard of Effingham*	
5671	*Prince Rupert*	Fitted with ash disposal device, c. 1942.
5672	*Anson*	Modified draughting 1957.
5673	*Keppel*	
5674	*Duncan*	
5675	*Hardy*	
5676	*Codrington*	
5677	*Beatty*	
5678	*De Robeck*	

NO	SELECTED NAME 1935/6	REMARKS
5679	*Armada*	
5680	*Camperdown*	
5681	*Aboukir*	
5682	*Trafalgar*	
5683	*Hogue*	
5684	*Jutland*	Fitted Kylchap double blast, 1936, removed 1938.
5685	*Barfleur*	Noted with 28 element superheater boiler, Feb 1955
5686	*St Vincent*	Carried 28 element boiler C 9207, Sept 1950—Jan 1954.
5687	*Neptune*	
5688	*Polyphemus*	Modified draughting 1957.
5689	*Ajax*	
5690	*Leander*	Still extant in scrapyard Sept 1970
5691	*Orion*	
5692	*Cyclops*	
5693	*Agamemnon*	
5694	*Bellerophon*	BR experimental livery, light green, 1948.
5695	*Minotaur*	
5696	*Arethusa*	
5697	*Achilles*	
5698	*Mars*	Fitted ash disposal device, 1939.
5699	*Galatea*	Still extant in scrapyard Sept 1970
5700	*Britannia*	Renamed *Amethyst* Sept 1951.
5701	*Conqueror*	
5702	*Colossus*	Fitted with ash disposal device, c. 1943.
5703	*Thunderer*	
5704	*Leviathan*	Last of class to run with Fowler tender exchanged 1964.
5705	*Seahorse*	
5706	*Express*	Badge below nameplate.
5707	*Valiant*	
5708	*Resolution*	Fitted with ash disposal device, c. 1943.
5709	*Implacable*	
5710	*Resolution*	
5711	*Courageous*	
5712	*Victory*	
5713	*Renown*	
5714	*Revenge*	
5715	*Invincible*	
5716	*Swiftsure*	
5717	*Dauntless*	
5718	*Dreadnought*	
5719	*Glorious*	
5720	*Indomitable*	
5721	*Impregnable*	
5722	*Defence*	Tested at Rugby Test Plant, autumn 1956/1957.
5723	*Fearless*	
5724	*Warspite*	
5725	*Repulse*	

NO	SELECTED NAME 1935/6	REMARKS
5726	*Vindictive*	
5727	*Inflexible*	
5728	*Defiance*	
5729	*Furious*	
5730	*Ocean*	
5731	*Perseverance*	
5732	*Sanspareil*	
5733	*Novelty*	Modified draughting 1957.
5734	*Meteor*	
5735	*Comet*	Rebuilt with large boiler and double chimney May 1942.
5736	*Phoenix*	Rebuilt with large boiler and double chimney April 1942.
5737	*Atlas*	
5738	*Samson*	Modified draughting 1957.
5739	*Ulster*	Coat of arms above nameplate.
5740	*Munster*	Dynamometer car tests Wolverhampton—Euston March/April 1937.
5741	*Leinster*	
5742	*Connaught*	Double Chimney removed Nov 1955.

The "M" prefix was used from February 2, 1948 to March 15, 1948 and the "4" prefix became valid from March 16, 1948.

The engines were 5XP until January 1, 1951 when they were reclassified 6P, they were reclassified 6P5F from Nov 1955.

The two engines rebuilt with the larger 2A boilers Nos 5735/6 were at first still 5XP, they were reclassified 6P in July 1943 and 7P on January 1, 1951.

Bibliography

"A Modern Locomotive Story", E. S. Cox, Paper presented to the Institution of Locomotive Engineers, January 2, 1946.

Locomotive Panorama, Vol 1, E. S. Cox, Ian Allan 1965.

Chronicles of Steam, E. S. Cox, Ian Allan 1967.

Sir William Stanier, O. S. Nock, Ian Allan 1964.

The British Railway Steam Locomotive Vol 2, 1925-1965, O. S. Nock, Ian Allan 1966.

Locomotive Liveries of the LMS, D. Jenkinson and R. J. Essery, Ian Allan 1967.

Various issues of:

Railway Magazine; Railways; Railway World; Trains Illustrated; Modern Railways; The Railway Observer; The Journal of the Stephenson Locomotive Society; The LMS Magazine.